REVIVAL COMES TO WALES

MAP of WALES
showing counties and
main centres of rev-
ival. Dates indicate
revivals prior to 1858

REVIVAL COMES TO WALES

The story of the

1859 REVIVAL IN WALES

EIFION EVANS

EVANGELICAL PRESS OF WALES

© Evangelical Press of Wales, 1959, 1967
First Edition (under the title **When He is Come**), 1959
Second Edition (published jointly with
Evangelical Press, London), 1967
Reprinted (with new title), 1979, 1982
Third Edition (with index), 1986
Reprinted 1991
Reprinted 1995

ISBN 1 85049 025 2

(Second Edition—ISBN 0 900898 42 9)

Cover picture: Courtesy of Jean Clement

Published by the Evangelical Press of Wales
Bryntirion, Bridgend, Mid Glamorgan CF31 4DX
Printed by Bridgend Print Centre
Tremains Road, Bridgend, Mid Glamorgan CF31 1UD

CONTENTS

". . . When he is come, he will reprove the world of sin, and of righteousness, and of judgment: of sin, because they believe not in me; of righteousness, because I go to my Father, and ye see me no more; of judgment because the prince of this world is judged . . . When he, the Spirit of truth, is come, he will guide you into all truth: for he shall not speak of himself; but whatsoever he shall hear, that shall he speak: and he will show you things to come. He shall glorify me: for he shall receive of mine, and shall show it unto you."

John 16: 8-14.

PREFACE

This study was first compiled for and delivered at a conference of ministers in June 1959. While the present form is somewhat expanded by the inclusion of additional material and the provision of notes, it is essentially the same as the papers read at that conference. The religious background of the 1859 Revival is briefly surveyed, and what could be considered formative and important elements are brought to the fore. Developments in the ecclesiastical sphere are traced leading up to the time of the revival. An outline of the rise, progress, and decline of the revival follows, the outstanding features being noted. Finally, an attempt is made to assess the achievements and fruit of the work.

Translations into English are not always verbally exact, but accuracy of representation has been consistently aimed at.

I am deeply grateful to my wife for her unfailing encouragement and patience. I am also greatly indebted to Mr. T. J. Hopkins, B.A., of the Research Department, Cardiff Central Library, for invaluable and untiring assistance; and to the Rev. Dr. D. Martyn Lloyd-Jones, London, for reading the manuscript.

EIFION EVANS

MEMORIAL HALL,
PRESBYTERIAN CHURCH OF WALES,
CARDIFF.
July, 1959.

PREFACE TO SECOND EDITION

Revision of this work has been mainly concerned with matters relating to typography and notes. With regard to the former many personal and place names not essential to the meaning have been omitted, and with regard to the latter only a few have been retained.

In addition to the persons whose help was acknowledged in the original Preface I have to add certain others. Chief among these is Mr. Robin Bird, of the Evangelical Press, whose painstaking corrections and helpful suggestions have been both wise and beneficial. I am under a similar obligation to the Rev. J. Elwyn Davies, B.A., and Miss Brenda Lewis, B.A., of the Evangelical Movement of Wales, not only for their part in the revision but also for their eager encouragement.

Above all I am thankful to God for this evidence of growing interest among His people in the reviving work of the Holy Spirit.

EIFION EVANS

First Presbyterian Church,
Carrickfergus.
June, 1967.

1. THE LAND OF REVIVALS

TO the vast majority of Welsh churches in 1859, revival was neither a new nor a strange phenomenon. Many of their members had witnessed previous manifestations of God's presence and power, even if they had not experienced them themselves. Consequently, when news reached Wales that a remarkable revival had broken out in America, most of the leaders in the churches were fully aware of the implications and effects of such a gracious, divine visitation. They were constrained to survey their own spiritual condition, and became gravely concerned at finding a serious deficiency in true godliness amongst the members, and an alarming ineffectiveness in the witness of the churches. As they applied themselves to prayer, they requested that God should do in their land what He had been pleased to do so many times before within living memory, and what He was doing at that time in America.

Another incentive to seek God for a renewed visitation of His Spirit in quickening the Church and in saving the ungodly was a knowledge of the historical facts and traditional records relating to the Methodist Revival of the previous century. This had been made available through the publication in the 1850s of the three-volume work by John Hughes, *Welsh Methodism*. By 1858 this would have been widely circulated and extensively read. Ever since about 1735 some Welsh locality or other had been the scene of a revival, which had stirred the churches and had brought about a radical change in the morals of the community. In 1858 the churches needed, and some of the most godly members amongst them desired, such another divine visitation.

9

The powerful influences of the first of these "Methodist" revivals were felt at Llangeitho under Daniel Rowland's ministry before 1740. At that time, the experience of gospel liberty was still very novel and fresh to Rowland, and the actual occasion when the remarkable movings of the Spirit were first experienced was while he was reading the Litany to his congregation. When he came to the words "By thine Agony and bloody Sweat; by thy Cross and Passion; by thy precious Death and Burial; by thy glorious Resurrection and Ascension; and by the coming of the Holy Ghost, Good Lord, deliver us", he was quite overcome by feelings of love, amazement and thankfulness. A similar sense of the Saviour's love overwhelmed the congregation, and many cried out in expressions of ecstasy and praise.

Another revival took place at Llangeitho under Daniel Rowland in 1762, on the occasion of the appearance in print of William Williams' collection of hymns bearing the title, *The Songs of those who stand on the Sea of Glass*. This awakening was especially noteworthy because of the spirit of exultation which pervaded the people and also because of its widespread effects. Furthermore, it cleared away much of the bitterness and malice over the separation and misunderstanding between Howel Harris and Daniel Rowland which had proved so lethal in many churches.

A succession of revivals

Between 1762 and 1862 there were at least fifteen outstanding revivals in Wales. Separately, each had its own characteristic, and together they served to justify, for that period at any rate, the appellation given to Wales of "the land of revivals". While some of these revivals were localised and geographically limited, others were far-reaching in their effects. In each of them were felt the most powerful influences of the Holy Spirit and the most amazing conversions were recorded. Many of the famous preachers of Wales attributed both their spiritual birth and their ministerial power to movings of the Spirit felt at such times. Robert Roberts, Ebenezer Morris and John Elias, for example, could look back with gratitude to God's gracious visitations in revival at Brynengan in 1785, Trecastle in 1786 and Bala in 1791, respectively.

The permanent effects of such awakenings therefore cannot be computed without assessing the influence of these men. Through the revivals, then, a great deal of good was felt not only by the particular church affected, nor merely at that particular time, but wherever such men eventually ministered, and for the length of time they were enabled to serve God in their generation.

For about a year before 1781 Daniel Rowland had been preaching on one theme. Towards the end of that period another amazing work of God broke out at Llangeitho. Similar outpourings of the Spirit were experienced at Crug-y-bar, Carmarthenshire, under the ministry of Isaac Price, the Congregationalist minister. In 1778 the Congregational church at Llanbryn-mair, Montgomeryshire, also tasted the sweet fruit of an awakening under the ministry of the famous Methodist exhorter and Congregationalist minister, Richard Tibbott. During the years 1784-5 places as far apart as Brynengan, in Caernarvonshire, and Twr-gwyn, in Cardiganshire, were greatly blessed. People of all ages felt the power of divine grace at Brynengan, and it was said of the work at Twr-gwyn that its effects were felt for some considerable time. Ebenezer Morris was but one of many whose lives were radically changed during the awakening at Trecastle in 1786. One, Mr. Bowen, of Pembrokeshire, was converted to Christ while travelling through the place, on hearing a young girl singing a hymn on the way home from chapel. He subsequently joined the Methodists and was an eminently useful

man in the church of his day. Reference has already been
made to Richard Tibbott. In 1787 the church of his charge
was blessed with another outpouring of the Spirit, the gracious
influences being quite irresistible, and as a result about ninety
were added to the church. Indeed, during Tibbott's ministry
at the church (1762-98) he received nearly 500 members into
fellowship.

Visitations in the 1790s

Hardly five years were to elapse before many widely
separated localities were again experiencing times of
refreshing from the presence of the Lord. Llangeitho was
blessed again with powerful divine manifestations towards
the end of 1790, about a month after the death of
Daniel Rowland. This work was characterised by the fact
that it received considerable stimulus from family worship.
Simultaneously, at Bala, Thomas Charles could also speak of
a revival, and in a letter dated January 26th, 1792, he writes of
the work, that it was ". . . *very gracious . . . very powerful
. . . growing . . . general . . . lasting . . .*" It had commenced in October 1791, when Thomas Charles was preaching
at the chapel in Bala on a Sunday. The Spirit's powerful
workings were felt particularly in the evening service: ". . .
about nine or ten o'clock at night", he says, "there was
nothing to be heard from one end of the town to the other,
but the cries and groans of people in distress of soul. And
the very same night, a spirit of deep conviction, and serious
concern, fell upon whole congregations, in this neighbourhood,
when calling upon the name of the Lord. In the course of
the following week, we had nothing but prayer meetings, and
general concern about eternal things swallowed up all other
concerns." Before the turn of the century, many places in
Cardiganshire, Carmarthenshire, Pembrokeshire, Caernarvonshire and Anglesey had been awakened. Thomas Charles,

John Elias, and Christmas Evans were instrumental in many of these awakenings. The experiences of divine grace and power were deep and lasting, and as a result, the morals of the people were raised, the means of grace were more esteemed, powerful and lively preachers were raised up in the churches, and there was a thirst for an intellectual and experimental knowledge of God.

Aberystwyth, 1805

The Aberystwyth revival of 1805 was first felt in the Sunday School, and received an added impetus from an Association of the Calvinistic Methodists held there at that time. The Sunday School had been established particularly through the labours of two young laymen, who later joined the Methodist church. One of them was to leave Aberystwyth, and at his farewell meeting, while engaged in prayer, "the Holy Spirit came upon him and the children so powerfully that the whole gathering became lost in tears and demonstrations". In a letter to the editor of the *Evangelical Magazine*, Thomas Charles describes the scenes he witnessed at Aberystwyth at that time:

"At Aberystwyth and in the adjacent parts, there are general and powerful awakenings among the young people and children. Some hundreds have joined the religious societies in those parts. I was there lately at an Association of the Calvinistic Methodists . . . The concourse of people assembled on the occasion was computed to amount at least to 20,000 . . . Hundreds of children, from eight years old and upwards, might be seen in the congregation, hearing the word with all the attention of the most devout Christian; and bathed in tears."

While there were several revivals in 1811 associated with the work of the Sunday Schools, the work at Tŷ-mawr, Lleyn, was chiefly among the older people. At about the same time, Llangeitho received yet another season of extraordinary blessing, referred to as the "quiet" revival because of the absence of such exultation and praising as had characterised previous revivals there.

Beddgelert, 1817

Several attempts have been made to describe adequately the powerful awakening at Beddgelert in 1817. Robert Jones claimed for it that:

"No one remembers seeing anywhere a more powerful owning of the means of grace than was experienced in this locality, and in many other places. The convictions were more powerful to awaken the conscience, smiting the heart, and the outbursts of the joy of salvation more powerful than were seen in some previous revivals."

To this, Robert Ellis merely adds succinctly, "And we know that there has been nothing comparable in *power* after it". D. D. Williams describes it as a "revival, the influence of which was profound, especially upon Caernarvonshire", while Edward Parry says that "previous to this, North Wales had not experienced such a powerful revival". The estimate of Henry Hughes is a generous one: "This revival is considered to be the most powerful ever experienced in Wales, unless it was the Methodist Revival in its first phases". Perhaps a more balanced estimate is that of Gomer M. Roberts, when he refers to it as "one of the most powerful visitations ever experienced in the North".

True religion had been at a low ebb at Beddgelert for some time before 1817. A barrenness was felt in the means of grace; the older Christians were indifferent, and the young people were worldly, and superficial in spiritual things. Meanwhile, at Nant chapel, in the Lleyn Peninsula, the Sunday

School superintendent was concerned with the lack of discipline amongst the children. He urged them to spend the time available between the means of grace on the Sabbath in prayer that the Lord would visit them by His Spirit. The spirit of prayer and supplications soon characterised the church members, as well as the children. It was not long before strong convictions were felt throughout the locality, and God's people were enabled to rejoice in God their Saviour. Shortly afterwards an elder related these incidents to the church at Beddgelert, so that, after years of spiritual dearth and moral darkness, the faithful of Zion were witnessing the desire of two or three to join with them in fellowship. This stirred them to seek God with renewed zeal, but the outcome of their prayers far surpassed their imaginations or desires. The next notable incident occurred in the Sunday School at Beddgelert. The young women of one of the Sunday School classes were moved to tears while reading a portion of St. John's Gospel. Further demonstrations of the Spirit's power were evident in the means of grace during the succeeding weeks, until the most powerful influences were felt, and the work spread abroad rapidly. The revival was experienced throughout North Wales, and certain parts of the South were also blessed. Some thousands were added to the church.

An unusual phenomenon in this revival was the "singing in the air" which many reliable witnesses had heard. The sound of heavenly, angelic voices, sweetly and softly joined in harmony, without any apparent melody, was overpowering. The effect on the hearer was to render him incapable of movement as though nailed to the spot. "One outstanding characteristic of the Beddgelert Revival," says Henry Hughes, "was that the preaching of the gospel had a prominent, indeed a predominant, place in it. In one revival, the most prominent feature is the prayer meeting; in another, it is the singing which has most influence; but it was preaching which had the leading part in this revival." During the years 1817-22 many parts of Wales were awakened, the work being by no means confined to the Calvinistic Methodists. The Baptists received more than 8,000 into membership between 1816 and 1822, and many Congregational churches in the counties of South Wales were blessed with revival.

Bontuchel, 1821

The revival of 1821 at Bontuchel, Denbighshire, broke out in a prayer meeting held on the first Monday of the month to pray for the world-wide success of the gospel. Those present were first stirred to a spirit of fervent praise and exultation while singing a verse of an old hymn by William Williams, which may be translated:

> O God, if Thou dost wish to end the world,
> First fulfil to the uttermost Thy Word;
>   Call Thine elect together
>   From all parts of the earth;
> Let the gospel sound reach every land,
> And wash multitudes in Thy blood,
>   And bring them true healing—
>   And then come down!

This was repeated several times until someone cried out aloud, unable any longer to restrain such strong emotions. This expression of ecstasy swept through the place like wildfire, and the congregation was as though electrified. The flame thus kindled spread rapidly, until many were "lost in wonder, love, and praise". The effects were extensive and lasting, and any hesitation or doubt on the part of the older saints as to the authenticity of the work was soon dispelled. The preaching of the Word became more powerful and authoritative; the church was thoroughly stirred up, and the most profligate sinners were converted. People praised God chiefly in verses taken from the Old Testament, a singular characteristic of this revival.

Anglesey, 1822

The Anglesey awakening in the following year, 1822, was one of the most powerful experienced on that island. The chief instrument used of God at that time was a young minister, Moses Jones, of Caernarvonshire, and the occasion on which the first movings of the Spirit in revival were felt was a preaching service. The large congregation present had gathered primarily in order to hear the famous Michael Roberts, but he had been unable to attend because of illness. However, the preaching of Moses Jones that night was "not with enticing words of man's wisdom, but in demonstration of the Spirit and of power". The whole island soon partook of the remarkable results of that meeting.

Carmarthen, 1828

The exercise of the ordinary means of grace was owned by God in the 1828 revival which commenced in Carmarthenshire. Early strong impressions of the divine power were felt at Llanddeusant during the prayer meeting, and especially while singing a hymn. The preaching of the Word was signally honoured during the following weeks, and the influences, which became more and more powerful, were experienced by adults and children alike. The work spread throughout the counties of South Wales. John Hughes estimates that about 280 were added to the church at Llanddeusant, and about 2,000 to the Calvinistic Methodist churches of the county, at that time. Many notable men amongst the Congregationals commenced their ministerial career as a result of this revival. Family worship received a tremendous stimulus from this work.

Caernarvon, 1832

Robert Dafydd, a preacher with the Calvinistic Methodists, had been praying for some years before 1832 that God would grant him the privilege of seeing yet one more revival. His prayer was answered, and the whole of Caernarvonshire felt the impact of an extraordinary manifestation of divine power. As a result, over six hundred were added to the church, apart from a considerable number of children. As a further preparation for this work of God, the most moving impressions were felt at the Pwllheli (Calvinistic Methodist) Association of September, 1831, while John Elias was preaching on Psalm 68: 1, "Let God arise, let his enemies be scattered . . ." Having faithfully and clearly described the low condition of the church, and having demonstrated unmistakably that God's presence and power were withdrawn from His people at that time, he urged Christians to give themselves to earnest and importunate prayer that God should again arise and visit Zion. The congregation was overcome with feelings of grief at this description of their state, and yet rejoiced that the sovereign God could still scatter His enemies. In the following year, Brynengan was among the first to be blessed with a mighty revival. About the same time, the locality of Llanystumdwy held its Sunday School Jubilee, and the revival broke out in the midst of those present with great power. Some fifty converts became members of the church within a short time, but the revival did not spread to other areas for quite a few months. The news that cholera had been reported in the North of England added a certain solemnity and gravity to the situation, and men became more concerned about eternal issues.

Merioneth, 1840

Two main reasons are put forward for denying the title of "revival" to the 1840 work. Firstly, because the application of Arminian principles was instrumental in bringing it about; and secondly, because it displayed no marked emotional agitation and disturbance, which had been so prevalent in previous revivals. Yet over two thousand were added to the churches in Merionethshire alone in 1840, and comparatively few of the converts fell away. The impact of this revival was felt in North Wales, in Liverpool, and in certain parts of South Wales. According to Thomas Rees, the means by which this revival was chiefly promoted was the reading and study of Finney's *Lectures on Revivals*. Consequently, believers were exhorted to pray and work for a revival, prayer meetings being held for this express purpose; "revival meetings" were held, and district evangelization was organised along lines suggested by Finney.

In this connection it is important to remember that the churches of that period were orthodox in their beliefs, and that, when they set themselves to seek God for revival, they would be drawing to a great extent upon lessons learnt in the revivals of the not so distant past. Henry Hughes mentions the Reverend B. W. Chidlaw of Ohio, who had come over to Wales from America, as being instrumental in commencing the work in North Wales. Further, the Congregational churches of Caernarvonshire had appointed the first of January, 1840, as a day of prayer for a religous awakening. Many places experienced great blessings by that exercise. Robert Ellis describes the principal features of this revival as "quiet and solemn", men considering well, and counting the cost, before they resolved to follow Christ.

South Wales, 1849

The great cholera epidemic which affected parts of South Wales in 1849 compelled many to think of their eternal welfare, and some thousands were converted during that and the following year. According to Thomas Rees, "No less than 9,139 were added to sixty-seven Independent churches in the counties of Monmouth, Glamorgan, Brecknock and Carmarthen, in the course of three or four months". He continues: "Many feared that an unusual number of relapses would follow this sudden increase, but their fears were not realised to nearly the extent it was apprehended".

A local revival at Henllan in 1850 was characterised by a spirit of sober self-examination, men proving themselves whether they were Christians or not, and earnestly seeking refuge in Christ.

There was also a "local" revival at Staylittle, Montgomeryshire, in 1851. Until this work, the means of grace were at a very low ebb, with hardly anyone able to lead and take part. A young man, David Vaughan, was greatly concerned about these things and urged his father to influence the faithful of the church in favour of a week of prayer meetings. No movement was felt during the first week; all was cold and lifeless, so that some advocated the termination of the prayer meetings. The following Tuesday night, however, while on their way home from the prayer meeting, the people heard the sound of singing, sweet and heavenly. News of this spread throughout the area, and during the next few days the Spirit's saving influences were strongly felt. The revival spread and many were added to the church.

Wales was thus stirred time and time again by such eventful revivals. They were periods of extraordinary spiritual activity, during which God drew near to His people and wrought the most amazing and revolutionary changes in numerous churches and amongst whole communities. The means used of God to commence and promote revival were the ordinary means of grace: the prayer meetings, the singing of the hymns of Zion, the sacrament of the Lord's Supper, the preaching of the Word and family worship. The far-reaching results of these revivals could not be estimated at the particular time of their occurrence, for they had repercussions far beyond the bounds of time and space. During such manifestations of the divine pleasure and grace the churches enjoyed singular blessings, not the least of them being the authority and success which attended the preaching of the Word.

Attention has been drawn, in the main, to the place and means of origin of these awakenings, but it is necessary to note that but few of the revivals dealt with were "local" and limited. For the most part, the revival would spread, from the actual church or locality where the influences were first experienced, to surrounding areas and even to neighbouring counties. The effects of some of them were felt throughout the Principality. They were, nevertheless, extraordinary times in the life of the Church. The general condition of the churches in the years preceding the 1859 Revival must now be examined.

2. THE TIME OF PREPARATION

DURING the last decade of the eighteenth century and the first four decades of the nineteenth, Wales had lost its most powerful, influential and outstanding preachers. Mention has already been made of Daniel Rowland's death in 1790; that of William Williams, followed in 1791, "so closely", says one writer, "that we may almost speak of them as a twin event". Williams died when South Wales was in the midst of revival, as has already been noted, and in his last letter to Thomas Charles he is able to report: "A great revival has taken place in many parts of our country—from 5 to 600, to my knowledge, have been added to the number of those who profess religion, during the last two years".[1] The Congregational minister, Edmund Jones of Pontypool, died in 1793, and Titus Lewis, the Baptist preacher and defender of Calvinism, died in 1811.

Welsh Methodism suffered great losses in the second decade of the nineteenth century: David Jones of Llan-gan, Thomas Charles of Bala and Thomas Jones of Denbigh, died in 1810, 1814 and 1820 respectively. Three famous men were enabled to carry on the living, vital tradition of vigorous, stirring preaching—Christmas Evans, William Williams of Wern and John Elias. They also entered into the theological debates of their time, Sandemanianism, Fullerism, Universal Redemption and the ever-present Arminianism. John Elias was one of the chief authors of the Calvinistic Methodist *Confession of Faith,* which was formulated in 1823 and published the following year. This doctrinal standard was based upon *The Westminster Confession of Faith,* and greatly

[1] See Note, p. 120.

influenced the Calvinistic Methodism of the period.[2] These three "stalwarts" of the Welsh pulpit died within three years of each other, Christmas Evans in 1838, William Williams of Wern in 1840 and John Elias in 1841.

The state of the churches

The 1859 Revival was the next major outpouring of God's Spirit in Wales after the death of these men.

During the intervening years, apart from the movements —chiefly local—in 1850, the churches had, by 1858, declined to an alarming state of deadness and barrenness. The means of grace had become more or less a formality, made unattractive to the world by the coldness even of its orthodoxy; sinful practices were rampant and carried on openly without any sense of shame; the Church was spiritually "asleep", oblivious of its mission to the world, and satisfied with its lukewarmness. The prayer meetings were not burdened for the souls of the unconverted, and preaching was theoretical, oratorical and "popular" in the worst sense. Thus E. Richardson writes in the *Drysorfa* for June, 1854: "We must confess that we have become too formal, lukewarm and unwilling in the work of the Lord generally in these days, but especially so in our prayer meetings". The same article, however, refers to the outstanding prayer meetings previous to the 1840 revival, and outlines the history of a local revival at Tunbridge Wells in April, 1854. The author concludes: "I hope that this synopsis of the events will have the right effect on the minds of many in Wales, to stir us up . . . from our stiffnecked and slumbering condition, and to apply anew to the Mediator urgently, longingly and earnestly seeking for a fresh outpouring".

By and large the churches were orthodox in their beliefs, but ineffective in their witness. Their orthodoxy is evident

[2] See Note, p. 120.

from the matters discussed at various Associations of the Calvinistic Methodists, for example—Bala, June, 1844: "The inefficiency of the ministry, and the low state of religion"; Denbigh, July, 1850: "Worldliness in its relation to religion"; Bala, June, 1855: "The ungodliness of the present generation". The subjects of the Association at Mold in March, 1847, are particularly interesting: "The obduracy (or hardness) of the times" and "The divinity (or divine authorship) of the Scriptures". Much concern was expressed at the Brecon Association of May, 1856, over the growth of "such a corrupt and deceitful system" as Mormonism in South Wales; "the recent attempts to desecrate the Sabbath by opening . . . public institutions"; and over "the attacks which are made on some of the fundamental truths of our religion, especially on the full inspiration and divine authority of the Holy Scriptures". There followed a renewed affirmation of allegiance to the article of the *Confession of Faith* relating to Holy Scripture, and a warning to the congregations in general, and to the young in their midst in particular, against such low and unworthy opinions regarding the "Book of the Lord".

Two items of relevance to this study appear in the *Drysorfa* for 1853. In the February issue John Hughes of Liverpool compares the Methodism of his own day with that of the turn of the century. He says:

"We must agree that the face of Methodism fifty years ago and before then is different from what it is now. There was more of an irresistible sharpness in the ministry; more solemnity in the convictions; the wheels of the religious machine turned faster; revivals were more frequent and more ardent; the experiences of the saints were sweeter, and their conversation more blameless."

The other item suggests a faint interest in revival. It is an extract from a Welsh-American periodical for April, and reads thus: "We do not remember hearing of religious awakenings in so many places . . . amongst our American fellow countrymen, than in the last two months. Must the Welsh nationals be as the mount of Gilboa in their midst?" In 1855 at least two men in Wales felt that the Spirit was preparing the country for great things. The Reverend David Charles, Principal of Trevecka College, said in the course of a sermon:

"There are signs which cause us to look for the breaking of the dawn again upon the cause of God amongst us. The watchmen of Zion are shewing symptoms of awakening. The ministry exhibits more life and earnestness than in times past, and I believe there is more praying. The breeze of the morning is already blowing, and we may expect the sun to rise before long . . ."

The name of David Morgan of Ysbyty Ystwyth is invariably linked with the 1859 Revival, not only because it was during this work that he rose to prominence, but also because he was eminently instrumental, under God, in promoting the revival, particularly in Cardiganshire. His diary for 1855 records:

"It is a big thing to have a feeling that God would revive His work. Whoever possesses such a feeling will be compelled to do all he can to revive the Lord's work. By reading the history of the Church we find that the great cause fluctuates up and down through the ages, but that, whenever the Lord drew near to save there was some considerable expectancy amongst the godly for His coming. As well as praying, we should be doing our utmost to revive the work. So did the godly of old: they prayed and they worked."

It is said of David Morgan "that for ten years before 1858 a petition for the outpouring of the Holy Spirit was never absent from his public prayers".

Towards the end of 1855 there was a spiritual awakening at the Congregational church of Capel Isaac, Carmarthen, on the coming of Rees Rees as their minister. These powerful impressions lasted for about two years, and between 150 and 200 were added to the church. Such movings of the Spirit were also felt at Trawsfynydd about that time. These were times when isolated cases of real progress in the success of the gospel were reported, as though the churches were being prepared, albeit in a small measure, for greater things.

The general religious situation

The religious situation in Wales in 1857 can be summed up as follows. The country had experienced great blessings in the past, particularly through the preaching of the Word. God had raised up men of singular gifts, and He had endowed them with tremendous power. They had been instrumental in creating and maintaining a religious awareness in Wales that could hardly be paralleled, and certainly not surpassed. There were many alive in 1857 who had seen great things in past revivals, and who had been brought to feelings of ecstasy and elation under the proclamation of the good news by great preachers.

The churches of the three main denominations were by and large orthodox, and militantly so, and there were indications amongst certain of the ministers of dissatisfaction as to the state of religion in the land. For in spite of past revivals, powerful preachers and present orthodoxy, a general apathy and indifference prevailed. This was coupled with a spiritual bankruptcy and stagnation, a lukewarmness and aridity, which were symptomatic of an almost apostate Church. The means of grace were neglected; there was much compromise with the world; there were petty grievances and jealousies within the churches; and the blight of traditionalism crippled much of the Church's young life and zeal—when men would speak of "the good old days" of bygone revivals, and lament for the preaching of the past. Men in their preaching sought to please their congregations by their oratory and display of knowledge, and in their reading they chose books which left them comfortably at ease in Zion. Those who made no profession of religion disregarded the Sabbath, the Church and the Word of God. Amongst such, there remained no vestige of interest in organised religion, and their profanity and boldness in sin knew no bounds.

There were, however, some gleams of light in this profuse and intense darkness. In the January 1857 issue of the Baptist magazine, *Seren Gomer,* there appears the following notice of a resolution passed at the West Glamorgan district meeting of December 1856: "Resolved . . . that the next meeting is to be held at Neath on January 7th and 8th. Mr. Williams of Salem to preach on the necessity for a religious awakening in the churches". Shortly afterwards the Reverend E. Richardson could write: "As I survey the scene, and look around me, I reckon that there is the dawn of hope for a religious awakening beginning to appear in several parts of the kingdom". He notes two things which cause him to entertain such a hope; one, that there is a feeling of brotherly unity amongst the denominations; and secondly, that God is raising up men of great ability and promise in the ministry— C. H. Spurgeon of London and Brownlow North of Scotland being two of the many he lists. The article is written, concludes Richardson, in the hope that it will be a means of urging God's people to be much and earnest at the throne of grace in seeking the spreading of an awakening throughout the land.

For the year ending June 1858, the Baptists in Glamorganshire could speak of an overall increase of 1,206 members, "in spite of all the wiles of the devil". At a meeting of the West Glamorgan Baptists held late in 1857, however, Mr. Phillips of Loughor preached on "The danger of religious

lukewarmness". These statements reflect a condition of un-
certainty and frustration in the churches. On the one hand,
the preaching of the Word was not without its effect, but on
the other hand, the churches were prone to be too readily
satisfied with a limited success. They failed to realise the
inadequacy of ordinary means to meet effectively the grave
situation which faced them.

A similar condition obtained for some time at Holyhead,
where a correspondent notes in 1859: "It is difficult to say
when the awakening actually commenced in the town, as
additions have been made to the churches week after week for
the last year or two. This increase has been very steady and
regular amongst the Independents for four years past."

The students at Trevecka, however, witnessed an "extraordinary manifestation of divine favour" during the winter of
1857. Here is an account of this work by one who was
present:

"Before separating (from the church meeting), our beloved
minister administered the sacrament of the Lord's Supper . . .
And in reading the Word of God, and making a few passing
remarks thereon, an influence was felt by all present, which
we had never experienced in the like manner before. There
was a beauty, a loveliness about the Holy Word which we had
never hitherto perceived. New light seemed to be thrown
upon it. It electrified us, and caused us to weep with joy.
The feeling became general. All present were under its influence. The hardest hearts were forced to succumb. After
some time we partook of the ordinance of the Lord's Supper,
but under strange emotions. And then we sang, ay, sang with
spirit, and repeated the hymn again and again—we could not
leave off. Every heart seemed inspired to continue, and the
last two lines were sung for full a quarter of an hour. Then
the minister prayed, and such a prayer we had never before
heard uttered. We felt that we were communing with God

. . . at length the prayer terminated, and we were to separate. But . . . every one resumed his seat and kept silence; and there we were for a length of time under the most heavenly feelings . . . At length the minister rose, and slowly and pathetically read several appropriate portions of the Word of God. We then sang, and afterwards prayed again. And thus the meeting was carried on for four hours."

Such deep spiritual experiences and such strong impressions were bound to influence not only the lives, but also the preaching, of those students present. Thus the same writer continues his testimony:

"The effects were not transient. They have left a deep impression on our minds, and have influenced our conduct for good. We feel more serious, more ready to speak about our religious life, more anxious as regards the salvation of the world, and more desirous that the Lord would dwell amongst us, and favour us with a still greater outpouring of His Holy Spirit."

In this way God was preparing men for an effective and edifying ministry in the time of revival, as well as subsequent to it. Doubtless, the Calvinistic Methodist churches, to which these students ministered during 1858, would have been at least challenged, if not stirred up, to seek God's face and a visitation of His Spirit in revival.

The American awakening stimulates concern

Meanwhile, in America, Jeremiah Lanphier had commenced a prayer meeting in New York on September 23rd, 1857, and had seen it grow during October in number and frequency. In November, Hamilton, Ontario, experienced some first-fruits of the revival which was soon to spread extensively throughout America. On December 1st a three-day convention was called at Pittsburgh under Presbyterian auspices to consider "the necessity for a general revival of religion in all the churches represented and others as well". Charles Hodge preached at the opening session of this convention on Zechariah 4: 6, "This is the word of the Lord unto Zerubbabel, saying, Not by might, nor by power, but by my spirit, saith the Lord of hosts". In the sessions which followed, the matters discussed included, firstly, the need for a religious awakening; secondly, hindrances to this; and thirdly, means to be exercised to secure such an awakening. The findings of the convention are both interesting and instructive. The ministers and elders present felt keenly

". . . the lack of unreserved consecration to the work of the Lord on the part of ministers, elders and Christian laymen; the unwillingness on the part of the churches to labour directly for the salvation of souls; lack of faith in the use of Sacraments; lack of faithfulness on the part of preachers for each other; conformity to the world and lack of a spirit of prayer amongst professors of religion; too close affinity with the things of the world; and many other things."

As to the means to be used to secure a revival, the following were noted:

". . . self-examination; repentance for sin; a vital faith in God's plan to save sinners and in His willingness so to do; persistent and importunate prayer for an outpouring of the Spirit; education in the truths of the Bible; direct effort on the part of Christians to bring others under the influence of the gospel; the faithful and practical preaching of the truth; together with complete dependence on the sovereignty of free grace for every success."

Similar matters were prominent in the minds of many Welshmen in the early months of 1858.

In the February 1858 issue of the *Annibynwr*, the Reverend W. Edwards of Aberdare, in an article on "Religious

Awakening", notes the desperately low condition of religion in those days. "There is need for a revival," he says, "a revival very soon, before things worsen, and go beyond recovery." He also puts forward some suggestions as to how a revival will be promoted. They include, "a pure ministry— apostolic preaching . . . the awakening must start in the pulpit . . . the church must be in full sympathy . . . with the ministry . . . the particular use of the means of grace . . . earnest prayer". The February issue of the Wesleyan Magazine, *Yr Eurgrawn Wesleyaidd,* carries the first of a series of articles on the same subject and makes much the same observations. The writer complains that, regarding revival, *"the Church and her ministers have capitulated to one of two extremes: Either to lean too heavily upon man, or otherwise to leave the work wholly to God"*. There were signs however that the churches were learning to lean more entirely upon God in personal dependence. Writing in March 1860, a correspondent of the Reverend Thomas Phillips records, ". . . about two years since, the churches became more earnest in prayer. God heard and answered".

About this time at Machynlleth the Congregational church under its minister, Josiah Jones, "was pervaded by a deep longing for a divine visitation . . . an additional prayer meeting . . . was kept up for nearly a twelve month, when the cheering news began to spread of the revival in Cardiganshire". Ebenezer Congregational church, Aberdare, had set its heart on securing a revival, and this "leaven" had been in the "lump" for a year before the revival broke out there early in April 1859.

The *Drysorfa* for April 1858 reports that American newspapers were publishing accounts of the awakening in New York, and this may well have inspired some churches to pray more fervently than ever before for a similar work in Wales. In the same issue Principal David Charles writes an article

on "The Promise of the Spirit", in which he examines the
contemporary situation. His assessment is a poor reflection
on the ministry at that time; nor is it any brighter regarding
the average church member.

"We come to the house of worship to listen to the preacher,
but not to expect succour from the message. We look for his
excellent, ornamental, masterly treatment, and seek to derive
entertainment for the mind from these things, rather than
feast upon the 'sincere milk of the word' . . . when the
emphasis is laid on the externals of the ministry, such as
voice and gifts, rather than on the substantial things, then
the ministry loses its authority and purpose, and the whole
thing takes on the nature of religious play-acting."

The remedy, concludes the writer, lies in prayer, personal
evangelism, ministerial application of the gospel in a personal
and direct manner, and a firm conviction and belief in the
authority of the Word of God.

It appears then, that during this period in Wales, in the
early months of 1858, there were churches which were being
challenged with a view of their own spiritual poverty and with
a call to earnest prayer. Evidence of this is provided in D.
Evans' *The Great Religious Revival in America; or God's
Triumph over Mammon in the New World in 1858,* which
appeared in print some time towards the end of 1858. The
author explains that, in the first place, the contents of the book
were delivered as a lecture to the people of his charge at
Aberaman on May 2nd, 1858. In the last chapter, he compares the American situation to that of Wales and finds an
almost exact correspondence. The coldness, deadness and
worldliness of the Welsh churches show that the need for
revival was paramount. The author concludes with his evalu-
ation of the means necessary to bring about this end:

"In order to be blessed with a similar gracious visitation

we must think of, and exercise the following things—1. *To repent and be humbled before God because of our sins . . . 2. The prayer meeting must have more attention from God's people; and the characteristics of their prayers must also change . . . 3. Christians must also make a personal effort, as well as pray in public . . . 4. There is every encouragement for God's people in their endeavours, and also for sinners to turn to the Lord."*

Furthermore, during April and May 1858, there were a number of remarkable local awakenings in Wales. At Llanfairfechan, the awakening commenced with the Wesleyans, who were, in January 1858, only twenty-four in membership. The church decided to be more at the throne of grace and to make the district the subject of prayer. A series of special preaching meetings was held from Monday to Thursday and strong impressions were felt, becoming more irresistible as the work went on. During the Sundays that followed the Spirit's influences were overpowering. All present would weep unashamedly, many crying out for mercy, and others praising God for the blood of Christ. By March, 134 had been accepted into membership after inquiry into their spiritual convictions. The Calvinistic Methodists also partook of the blessing, and in the same period, sixty were added to their church. The revival spread to neighbouring towns and villages such as Conway, Llandudno, Aber, and even as far as Pwllheli.

The first movings of the Spirit at the Congregational church at Llangybi, Cardiganshire, were felt in a preaching service. Powerful convictions were felt by the congregation about half-way through the Sunday afternoon service of April 17th and many gave vent to their feelings in tears. As a result, prayer meetings were commenced, and were held by rotation in farms and dwelling houses in the locality. Soon the houses became too small, and many prayer meetings were held simultaneously in many parts of the area, extending to Silian, Abermeurig, Llangeitho, Tregaron and Llanddewibrefi. Family worship, hymn-singing, Bible reading, church attendance and salvation soon became the leading topics of the day. Many were added to the church, and powerful impressions had been felt for some time before news of a similar work at Ysbyty Ystwyth reached the area.

The *Diwygiwr* for May 1858, draws the attention of its readers to the American revival, and then proceeds to report certain movements of the Spirit felt amongst a number of Congregational churches at that time. Some tens of people had been converted in and around Swansea; nine had been received into membership at Tre-lech, and thirty at Llwynhwrdd. The dawn had also broken at Wern, Aberavon, where a number had joined the fellowship. The notice concludes: "This is a great encouragement and a strong incentive for us to seek an even fuller and more powerful outpouring of the Holy Spirit". Thomas Edwards had been inducted minister of the Congregational cause at Ebenezer, in the parish of Llanddeiniolen, Caernarvonshire, in July 1832. Five years passed before he saw any appreciable success in his ministry, but in 1837 a powerful revival broke out in the church and many were converted. A new chapel was opened in May 1851, which Thomas Edwards feared would be too large for it ever to be filled. In 1858, however, another visitation of divine power dispelled his doubts, as many were again added to the church. Nevertheless, looking back on this work in 1859, he says: "The revival of last year was only like John the Baptist intimating that one stronger than he was close at hand". These instances of local revivals, at places as widely separated as Llanfairfechan, Llangybi, Swansea, Aberavon and Ebenezer, serve to demonstrate the longing in some quarters for an effective remedy to a situation which was already alarming, and which showed signs of gradual deterioration. Such minor eruptions were but the precursors of that momentous upheaval, born of nothing less than an extraordinary divine visitation, which came to be known as "the '59 Revival".

God's people stirred to earnest prayer

Several events occurred in the summer of 1858 which assume great importance and significance in the light of the revival. In the April Association of the Calvinistic Methodists at Aberystwyth attention had already been drawn to the religious revival in America, "as well as in certain parts of this country", and these observations had been followed by a discussion on "the necessity for the work of the Spirit to secure a religious awakening". The North Wales Association held at Holywell in June discussed "Religious Awakening", and the *Drysorfa* gives an account of the proceedings:

"It was noted that there was much discussion in these days on religious awakening. The reports given of the revival in America, and in a few outstanding places in this country, have instigated no small disturbance throughout the churches generally; and it is hoped that this is an intimation that a great and general revival is at hand . . . *What is meant by religious awakening? . . . Have we any reason to expect a religious awakening? . . . Have we anything to do in order to secure a religious awakening?* . . . Hearing of a religious awakening in other lands creates a desire to see it in our own midst and the desire for it is a good preparation to receive it. Let it be much in our discussion; and let us apply to God in diligent prayer to seek it."

The influence of such Associations would be quite widespread, since reports of the deliberations and resolutions would be taken back to the various presbyteries represented for further consideration and application by the churches.

Just over two weeks before the Holywell Association, the
Baptists of Monmouthshire, at their Assembly held in May,
had obviously been discussing much the same matters, for it
was "Proposed by Dr. Davies, and seconded by the Rev.
Owen Williams—'That the first Sunday in August should be
spent by the churches in prayer for a more extensive outpouring of the Holy Spirit upon them'." On June 14th, the
Congregationalists of Monmouthshire held their Quarterly
Meeting at Pen-y-waun, and some of the resolutions passed
are an echo—if not an outcome—of the Baptist Conference
held the previous month in the same county. An account of
this meeting appeared in the *Diwygiwr* for July, and reads
as follows:

"We had a very profitable and edifying fellowship meeting
on the signs of an awakening in religion evident in these days
in some places, and that we should take note of this, so that the
awakening should become more general. The Conference
unanimously recommended . . . That the first Sabbath of
next August should be set aside to hold prayer meetings
throughout all the churches of Monmouthshire, and as many
other counties of Wales as will see fit to join us in this
important matter."

The Congregational churches of at least three other counties in South Wales did see fit to join those of Monmouthshire
"in this important matter". They resolved to do so at the
Four-Counties Assembly at Aberdare on June 23rd and 24th,
the Reverend Ellis Hughes proposing that the Assembly
should make such a recommendation to the churches, in view
of the powerful revivals in America, and the adoption already
by the Monmouthshire churches of such an arrangement. The
proposition was seconded by William Griffiths of Llanharan,
who expressed his sincere hope that the churches "would pray
much between now and then for a spirit and faith appropriate

to that great and important work". He went home after this Assembly at Aberdare, "and stated the resolution" to his people, with the result that "some unusual feeling thrilled through the minds of all present". He continues:

"When the stated Sabbath arrived, we were blessed with remarkable earnestness at the throne of grace for the descent of the Holy Spirit to revive the Church and convert the world. Ever since that memorable Sabbath, the prayer meetings presented a new aspect—they gradually increased in warmth and number during the following months. This continued to February [1859] . . . when it pleased Jehovah to pour down His Spirit from on high, as on the day of Pentecost."

Evan Jones of Crug-y-bar, Carmarthenshire, bears witness to a similar blessing resultant upon that Sunday's prayer meetings. "I believe," he says, "there has been more prayer for this great blessing [the outpouring of the Holy Spirit] ever since." Thus, many churches, responding to such directives from their ecclesiastical courts, set themselves to pray for an outpouring of the Spirit.

Other churches too were pervaded with a spirit of prayer and a sense of need, the incentive or stimulus being generally the news of the American Revival. The reports of the American work which continually appeared in the religious periodicals of the time served as fuel to the fire until in many quarters there was a feverish longing after God, and for a manifestation of His presence amongst His people. William Jenkins, minister of Rehoboth Congregational church, Bryn-mawr, speaks of his experience, and in doing so, provides a typical example of the experience of many others:

"Ever since the news of the outpouring of the Spirit upon the American churches reached our country, I longed and prayed that the Lord would, in his infinite mercy, visit poor Wales. I immediately brought the subject before the church

and earnestly exhorted them to 'seek the Lord' . . . I related
every fact and incident I could glean . . . in order to produce
in the minds of my people the desire of a similar visitation
. . . Some of (our aged members) . . . prayed as I have never
heard them pray before. A new burden seemed to press on
their hearts . . . There were no less than eighty-five added
to the church in about six months after those prayer meetings.
This was in the year 1858."

These prayer meetings at Bryn-mawr lapsed after a period
of time, but restarted on hearing of the revival in Cardiganshire, and were further stimulated by news of the revival in
Ireland.

The experience of Hermon (Calvinistic Methodist) chapel,
Mynydd Llandygái, in Caernarvonshire, was remarkably
similar. A correspondent of the *Drysorfa* for December 1859,
gives the details:

"Having heard of the great upheaval which had taken
place in the courts of Zion's daughter in America, when the
Saviour's cause was raised, as it were, from death to life there,
it came to the mind of the Lord's people in this place to hold
a meeting for prayer once a week; and the particular subject
of the prayers was to plead that God would also visit them in
the influences of His Spirit, as comforter and convicter. This
meeting was quite popular for a while; but somehow or other
it gradually diminished, until the attendance at the gatherings
was very low."

Here also the prayer meeting received new life upon hearing of the revival in Cardiganshire, increasing considerably
in a sense of earnestness and urgency as the revival came
geographically nearer. The dawn finally broke in the young
people's Sunday night prayer meeting where, under the influence of the Spirit, some prayed for deliverance, others wept
bitterly and others praised God for having at last visited His

people. This went on for some hours, and proved to be the first-fruits of a mighty awakening which soon spread to neighbouring churches.

This conviction of the efficacy of prayer to meet the grave situation which faced the churches seems to have been quite widespread, and instances of this could be multiplied. Three more, however, must suffice. At Abertrinant, near Towyn, an elder of the Calvinistic Methodist cause was concerned about the condition of the church, and influenced the members to hold a meeting on Sundays at 8 a.m. in order to pray for the success of the gospel. The time of the prayer meeting was changed to 1 p.m. as the days grew shorter, but, in spite of occasional blessings felt during these meetings, they eventually ceased. The same elder, on hearing of the awakening in Cardiganshire, urged that the prayer meetings should be restarted. After some weeks of ordinary, uneventful meetings, the faithful ones began to feel the strong influences of the Spirit at work, until an unusually powerful movement was felt early in March 1859. From that Sunday night, when every one present had been moved to tears and cries in the Spirit, till the end of May when the report was submitted for publication, the revival continued to stir and inspire. Weekly prayer meetings had been started at Nantmor, near Beddgelert, since April 1858, while the Wesleyan church at Brymbo, Denbighshire, had made the salvation of sinners the special subject of the most earnest prayer since the end of 1858.

These facts clearly indicate that God was preparing His church for the extraordinary manifestation of His Spirit which reached its peak in 1859. Prayer meetings such as those mentioned were neither infrequent nor ineffective. They may have appeared at the time as isolated and weak attempts to secure the desired end, but viewed historically and collectively they are seen to be essential elements in the pattern which was being wrought in the good providence of God. During the early months of 1858 the awareness of revival, particularly the need for it in Wales, was coming more and more into focus. The summer months brought news of the American Revival, which presented not only an invigorating challenge, but also a tried remedy, that of prayer. By the closing months of that year very many of the Welsh churches had applied themselves to diligent and fervent prayer for revival, so that what has been said of the Ulster Revival of 1859 is also true of the Welsh Revival, it was born in prayer.

In many cases churches were moved to prayer upon a consideration of the American work, and after hearing of it. John T. Carson, in his recent book on the religious awakening of Ulster in 1859, concludes that "There is no reasonable doubt that the Ulster awakening owed much to the dissemination of news of the American Revival . . . It is also an historical fact that consideration of God's mighty works in by-gone days creates a longing for similar evidences of the Holy Spirit's presence among His people". This is equally true of Wales, for, as a result of hearing or reading accounts of the work in America, and afterwards in Cardiganshire, many churches felt acutely their own need and set themselves to sue God for similar manifestations of His power. The Reverend D. Edwards testified, "I am persuaded that the means blessed of God to create and carry on the revival in *most* places, if not in *all*, is *prayer*. You can trace its origin and progress, in every locality, to prayer, especially the prayers of the new converts, after they have commenced their career."

The 1859 Revival in Wales was also indebted to the American work for another reason. Humphrey Rowland Jones, formerly of Tre'r-ddôl, near Aberystwyth, followed his parents to America in 1854, and had been ordained to the Wesleyan ministry there. He had been greatly blessed and used in the American awakening, his inspired ministry being eminently successful among the Welsh settlers in America.

He returned to Wales with the express intention of spreading the revival fire in his native land. In God's sovereign purpose, his arrival at his old home towards the end of June 1858, precipitated that gracious manifestation of the Spirit's work which soon engulfed the whole of the Principality in a powerful revival.

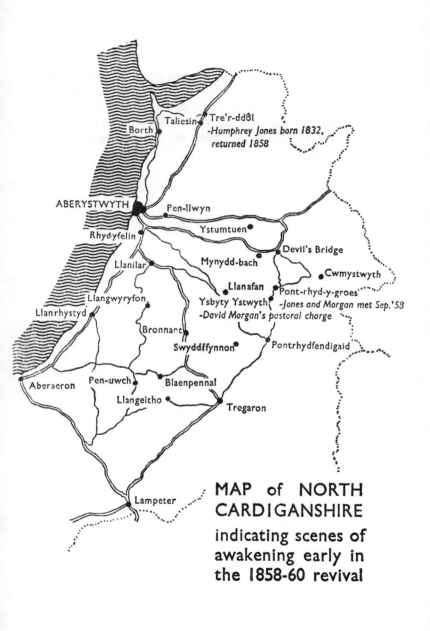

Tre'r-ddôl
-Humphrey Jones born 1832,
returned 1858

Taliesin
Borth
ABERYSTWYTH
Pen-llwyn
Rhydyfelin
Ystumtuen
Llanilar
Mynydd-bach
Devil's Bridge
Cwmystwyth
Llanafan
Llangwyryfon
Pont-rhyd-y-groes
Llanrhystyd
Ysbyty Ystwyth
-Jones and Morgan met Sep.'53
Bronnant
-David Morgan's pastoral charge
Swyddffynnon
Pontrhydfendigaid
Aberaeron
Pen-uwch
Blaenpennal
Llangeitho
Tregaron

Lampeter

MAP of NORTH
CARDIGANSHIRE
indicating scenes of
awakening early in
the 1858-60 revival

3. THE MEN OF VISION

A N indication has already been given that the 1859 Revival in Wales came to churches which were in many ways conditioned for it. The influence of the denominationally sponsored prayer meetings for revival and discussions upon it, together with that of the appearance of religious intelligence regarding the American awakening, must have been quite widespread. As a result, many churches had become grossly dissatisfied with the deadness and barrenness of their spiritual condition, and they were pervaded with a sense of longing for a supernatural intervention of the divine grace. Reference has already been made to the Holywell Association of June 1858, and to the commencement of prayer meetings at Abertrinant in Merionethshire. J. J. Morgan gives the exact nature of the directive issued from that Association regarding revival, and in doing so, shows its relationship to the prayer meetings at Abertrinant:

"In June 1858, a message came from the Holywell Association that the churches should earnestly seek a religious awakening, and should purge out the hindrances thereto from their midst. After receiving the above message a special prayer meeting was commenced at 8 o'clock on Sunday morning. This soon dwindled, but was re-started when the news was received that the Lord was walking in His garden in north Cardiganshire, and making His paths resplendent. The first Sunday in March 1859, they understood that 'the day of visitation, the blessed day, promised of the Father' was come. At the end of the Sunday night prayer meeting, 'every one called upon his God, every heart was wounded sore, and every face rivers of tears'. Ten were added (to the church) that night."

The blessings of revival at Abertrinant, and in many other places, were thus felt independently of a visit from David Morgan, or any other revivalist. It was true, therefore, that one of the characteristics of the 1859 Revival in many areas was that it had no acknowledged or predominant leader. While David Morgan was extensively used, the revival of 1859 cannot be equated with, nor confined to, the limits of his influence and work.

"The individuals who have been chiefly instrumental in the commencement and spread of the work . . . have been men more distinguished for their piety, zeal, love of God and compassion for souls, than for high attainments and intellectual powers . . . the absence of great names, while at the same time a great and mighty spiritual work has been done, will the more effectually secure the glory to Him who alone gives the increase."

So testifies Thomas Phillips, and J. Edwin Orr draws upon *The Revival* for a parallel statement, to the effect that "the Welsh Revival of 1859 was independent of great personalities". He concludes, "Even David Morgan the revivalist, who was signally used in the inception and spread of the movement, was a simple country pastor". Nevertheless, in God's providential ordering, certain men were granted a unique vision and, urged forward by this vision, they served God and His Church faithfully, and therefore they rose to some prominence at that time.

Humphrey Jones

Humphrey Rowland Jones was undoubtedly one of these "men of vision". Born at Tre'r-ddôl, near Taliesin, Cardiganshire, in 1832, he recounts his early spiritual career in this way:

"I was received a member of the church when I was only ten years of age. When I was fifteen, I experienced deep, stormy and poignant convictions, which lasted for seventeen months. 'I was sore broken in the place of dragons.' At that time, when I was sixteen years of age, before emerging from the period of conviction, it was urged upon me that I should commence preaching, and this I did, more from obedience to others than from my own inclination. Seventeen souls were convicted under my third public sermon, on the words, 'And if the righteous scarcely be saved, where shall the ungodly and the sinner appear?' (1 Peter 4: 18). At Ystumtuen twelve were converted; eight or nine at the close of a service at Mynydd-bach. I have reason to believe that the Lord of His grace blessed my ministry at that time to the salvation of some hundreds of souls in the upper reaches of Cardiganshire."

He subsequently applied for admission to the Wesleyan ministry, but was rejected, probably because there was no call for preachers in that year. Resolved to preach in spite of this difficulty, he emigrated to America in 1854, some seven years after his parents. Having preached to the Welsh settlers in New York for a year, he was ordained deacon by the Episcopal Methodists, and appointed missioner to the Welsh community at Oshkosh, Wisconsin. He laboured here for the space of a year, and broke off relations with the Episcopal Methodist Conference towards the end of 1856, thereby being enabled to preach where and when he desired.

Cambria, Wisconsin, was one of the first places of his choice. According to his own testimony, it was here that he first laboured as a revivalist, his successes at Cambria being followed by even greater ones as he moved from place to place, preaching amongst the Welsh communities. While the first movings of the American Revival were not felt until early October 1857, Humphrey Jones had begun his work as revivalist soon after his resignation from the Episcopalian Methodists, probably during the spring months of that year. He conducted missions in many places, and amongst churches of various denominations, gradually working his way eastwards to New York, and he soon became known as "Humphrey Jones the revivalist".

Here is his own account of that period of his life, and the success which attended his ministry:

"The place where I first laboured as revivalist was Cambria, Wisconsin. Twenty-one stayed behind after the first meeting of the series, that is, all but one of the number present . . . I remained in those parts for about a month. Then I came to the Oshkosh area, where I laboured for a fortnight . . . Thence I went to Waukesha institute, and it was there that the great dawn and the most powerful revival of my ministry in America broke out. Then I went to the city of Milwaukee: I was at the same place there every night, and thrice on a Sunday, for over a month. I saw there some of the most remarkable meetings I have ever witnessed. Forty-five were converted. After that, I spent a month at Racine, and a fortnight at nearby Pike Grove. In spite of the fact that it was the time of harvest, the people came together to pray at six o'clock in the morning, as well as at night. From those parts I went to Big Rock, Illinois. I was there for three weeks, preaching to Welsh and English congregations. I received an invitation to the yearly meetings of the Wesleyans in the Oneida Province of New York. There I began a series of revival meetings among the several denominations. At that time in Oneida about seven hundred souls were converted. On the way to Wales, I stopped at New York, where I occupied the pulpit of John Ellis, who was ill, and over forty were converted under my ministry."

With these rich and profound spiritual experiences, Humphrey Jones returned to Wales with the express purpose of bringing the revival to his native land. Having arrived at Liverpool towards the end of June 1858, he stayed with the Wesleyan minister, William Jones, to whom he mentioned that he purposed to hold revival meetings at Aberystwyth and the surrounding districts. On the first Sunday morning after his arrival at Liverpool, he preached at the Wesleyan chapel in Benn's Garden, but was unable to minister in the evening because of bodily weakness.

After arriving at his native village he visited the homes of friends and offered prayer, and it was evident to all who joined in the family worship that remarkable power and pathos attended his prayers. The Sunday following he ministered there, and possibly at Eglwys-fach, some three miles away, in the afternoon. His texts were, Amos 6: 1, "Woe to them that are at ease in Zion"; Revelation 3: 16, "So then because thou art lukewarm, and neither cold nor hot, I will spue thee out of my mouth"; and Jeremiah 7: 24, "But they hearkened not, nor inclined their ear, but walked in the counsels and in the imagination of their evil heart, and went backward, and not forward". During the week which followed prayer meetings were held each night at Tre'r-ddôl, at the end of which, Humphrey Jones would urge sinners to trust in Christ. During the second week "the revivalist preached, and weeping converts sought peace at every service". By August 7th, a correspondent of the *Herald Cymraeg* could report of the revival meetings, that his ministry was "very powerful", and that in one month fifty had joined the church.

His method and success are described in a letter by him to the following week's issue of the *Herald*, and it provides an interesting picture of the beginnings of the 1859 Revival in Wales:

"The sound of revival is quite foreign in Wales in these days. Religion is at a very low ebb throughout the land, the prayer and fellowship meetings are lifeless and poorly attended. Such was also the case in this locality; but five weeks ago I happened to come home from America to visit my relations, and as the friends heard about the mighty revival in America, and saw my name in conjunction with the awakening in some publications, they felt a keen desire that I should apply the same plan in this locality: we did this and the effect was remarkable. The church was thoroughly awakened, and prayer meetings were held every night. At the conclusion of the prayer meeting, I would ask whether there were some sinners present who desired a part in the prayers of the church and who wished to give themselves to the Saviour. Should there be any such, they were urged to come forward to the altar . . . During the second week, there was preaching every night, and some came forward at the end of every service. Fifty-one have been converted in this locality up to the present. This is regarded as a major revival in such a small congregation and in such a sparsely-populated area. The revival continues. The movement has proved influential far and near. I receive letters from all directions requesting that I should go there and hold similar meetings . . . I believe that Wales is on the brink of blessed things, and that revivals will be commonplace happenings throughout the land."

This conviction, that Wales was about to experience such a gracious visitation of the Holy Spirit, was reiterated in a letter to Lewis Ellis, then a student at Bala, of whose preaching at nearby Taliesin he had heard encouraging reports. In that letter, Humphrey Jones' chief purpose was to seek Lewis Ellis' fellowship and companionship in the work of spreading the revival, and the revivalist noted two things necessary in order to be a successful preacher.

". . . for one thing, to be a man of fervent prayer in secret; to be there several times a day, wrestling with God; each time as though it were the last; refusing to get up from your knees until an earnest had been given that the Lord had heard; asking the Lord in faith and with importunity what to say to the people; going straight from the secret-place into the pulpit each time . . . The other thing is to preach with severity and conviction; aiming continually at the conscience; charging the people with their sins to their very face; having no regard for men's good or bad opinions; and avoiding the exhibition of self during the delivery of your sermon."

His mission at Tre'r-ddôl lasted for five weeks, during which time the revival spread to the neighbouring towns and villages. A preaching festival was held at Bont-goch, some five miles away, towards the end of that period, and it was attended by large numbers of people. Humphrey Jones was to be the third speaker at the evening service. Throughout the day, and in the evening, there was a spirit of hardness and heaviness upon the congregation, but when he gave out the hymn

> "Life of the dead, come into our midst,
> And by Thy Spirit breathe upon us,"

a strange influence was felt by all present, so that the hymn was repeated several times over. Humphrey Jones then preached on Ephesians 5: 14, "Awake thou that sleepest, and arise from the dead, and Christ shall give thee light". One witness described the scene which followed as "a second Pentecost", for before the preacher had finished his closing prayer, "scores of people were praying aloud, until the preacher's voice was drowned".

The revivalist went to Ystumtuen early in August, and remained there for a month, following much the same procedure as at his home village. His basic principle in seeking revival was to awaken the church, before launching an attack upon unbelief and wickedness. This radically influenced his methods, and his initial, urgent message to the church was that she should herself be stirred from her condition of ease, slumber and apathy. This is evident from the texts of his sermons, but this method also proved a singular blessing to the unconverted within and without the church. Some at Ystumtuen, as at other places, were prejudiced against the revivalist because of his youth; others were biased against the denomination to which he belonged. Nevertheless, his work was crowned with success, the most hardened and hopeless men feeling the strongest convictions, which often prevented sleep and work alike for greater or lesser periods, but subsequently finding peace in a crucified and risen Saviour. After three weeks' preaching to the church, and personal visitation of those who never attended a place of worship, Humphrey Jones could report to the *Herald Cymraeg,* that seventy-six had already been converted, of whom there were real evidences that their profession was well-founded. Before the end of September, he had been to Mynydd-bach, near Devil's Bridge, holding prayer meetings and experiencing similar blessings. On September 30th he commenced his mission at Pont-rhyd-y-groes, where David Morgan heard him for the first time. Jones' successes during this time are summed up by J. J. Morgan as follows: 140 converts at Tre'r-ddôl and Taliesin in the first month; 100 at Ystumtuen in the second month; forty at Mynydd-bach in the third month; 150 at Pont-rhyd-y-groes in the fourth month; and fifty at Cnwch-coch and Cynon in the fifth month.

David Morgan

David Morgan first came under spiritual convictions in 1836 when he was twenty-two years of age. It was not until some months had passed that he was delivered from the bitter sense of guilt and condemnation, and experienced the full power of the gospel, under the ministry of Evan Evans at Cwmystwyth. At that time he was working as a carpenter, but because of the intense feeling and wealth of his prayers, he was urged to preach. This external call from some brethren in the faith was confirmed by an inward call from God, which he received at a time of revival in 1841. Eighteen months later he was eminently blessed and used in a local revival in Cardiganshire, but he lost his "first love" shortly after this amazing work. He was accepted as candidate for the ministry by the Llangeitho Association of 1848, even though he refused to promise that he would go to college. It is said, however, that in his sermon preparation, he was helped by studying such works as James Hughes' *Commentary on the Bible*; a Welsh translation of Thomas Watson's *Body of Divinity*; and John Owen's *Works* in English, with the help of his brother William to translate and clarify certain difficult words. David Morgan went on two preaching tours through North Wales before the revival, the one in June 1849, and the other in March 1855. He was ordained to the full work of the ministry at the Trevine Association on May 20th, 1857, but it was not until March 1868 that he was given the official call to be pastor of the church at Ysbyty Ystwyth.

Before Humphrey Jones' visit to Pont-rhyd-y-groes, David Morgan had been suspicious and uncertain regarding the work done by the young Wesleyan revivalist from America. According to Edward Thomas, writing in 1897, Morgan "was strongly opposed to the 'revival', and full of prejudice, which was apparent to all". Thomas Edwards, minister of the Calvinistic Methodist church at Pen-llwyn, Cardiganshire, in an article to the *Drysorfa* for April 1859, on "The Religious Awakening in Cardiganshire", confessed of David Morgan and himself, that neither of them was entirely free from prejudice against the work, until their fears about Humphrey Jones' methods were dissipated.

Morgan was present at Jones' first revival meeting at Pont-rhyd-y-groes on September 30th, but took no part in it, being content to listen and estimate the authenticity of the work. Humphrey Jones preached on 2 Samuel 19: 11, "And king David sent to Zadok and to Abiathar the priests, saying, Speak unto the elders of Judah, saying, Why are ye the last to bring the king back to his house? seeing the speech of all Israel is come to the king, even to his house". He followed his usual procedure, the sermon being a call to the church to awake out of her apathetic slumber, and the address after the sermon, when he had descended from the pulpit, being directed to the unconverted in an earnest and moving manner. The following night, he preached with conviction on Revelation 3: 16, and David Morgan became acutely aware of the shortcomings of his own ministry in the face of the dire need of the church in those days. Later that night, he sought out Humphrey Jones, convinced that the Holy Spirit Himself was the author of this singular and powerful work.

"They conversed for hours about the forlorn condition of Zion, and Mr. Jones insisted that it was due to the drowsiness and supineness of the watchmen on its walls. At last David Morgan said, 'There can be no harm in our attempting to rouse the churches of this region; I am willing to do my best. We can do no mischief by holding prayer meetings, though there should be no more than *man* in it all'. 'You do that,' responded the other, 'and I will guarantee that *God* will be with you very soon'."

During the whole of the following day, October 2nd, 1858, David Morgan was found alternately at the throne of grace, wrestling with God in prayer, and in company with Humphrey Jones seeking his guidance and counsel. Such was the turmoil in his mind concerning the tremendous issues of the lukewarmness of the church, the inefficiency of his own ministry, and the remarkable power of God already manifested in the awakening of God's people in America and at Tre'r-ddôl, that he was unable to fulfil his preaching engagement at Soar on the Sunday morning of October 3rd. Instead, he attended the service at Ysbyty Ystwyth where Humphrey Jones was ministering. The preacher's message was based upon Amos 6: 1, and it was delivered with a sense of urgency and solemnity, but the atmosphere was cold and the congregation unresponsive. J. J. Morgan gives an account of the church meeting which followed.

"The preacher complained rather bitterly of the frigidity of the religious atmosphere, and turning to the elders, said, 'Not one of you helped me with so much as an "Amen".' One of them . . . rose, and replied, 'It is very difficult for a man, when the ministry condemns him, to cry "Amen" with it.' Overcome by sudden feeling, the old man burst into tears, and fell into his seat as if in a swoon. He was a man of undoubted piety, and unfailing faithfulness in all departments of Christian work; and when *he* was heard acknowledging his guilt in the face of the sermon, the entire church was struck by an overwhelming wave of emotion, and, as if by a simultaneous impulse, every face was bowed low and bathed in tears."

That evening David Morgan preached at Ysbyty on Matthew 25: 10, "they that were ready went in with him to the marriage: and the door was shut". During the service an announcement was made that prayer meetings would be held each night of the coming week alternately at the Wesleyan and Calvinistic Methodist churches. He preached twice at Llangurig on the Monday, and his son records the important and significant experience of the Tuesday night on his return:

"Not yet had he received power from on high, and as he hurried home to the united prayer meeting arranged for Tuesday evening, his bosom was agitated by intense and conflicting emotions. Though he had sought the blessing for years, he was abashed when he realised that it was at hand, awaiting his acceptation. He retired to rest at his usual time on Tuesday evening, and slept for some hours. He awoke about 4 a.m., and was instantly conscious that some strange, mysterious change had come over him. He became aware with awe of a marvellous illumination of his faculties, especially of his memory. 'I awoke about four in the morning,' said he himself, 'remembering everything of a religious nature that I had ever learnt or heard'."

The added keenness given to his memory at this time became proverbial while the flames of the revival burned, and remained an evidence of the Spirit's equipment to this man of God for several months. The same source continues:

"Congregations were filled with amazement during the coming months, when they heard him pray for dozens of converts and their relatives, each one by name; recapitulating in his intercessory prayer on their behalf, not only their names, in the order that he had spoken to them as they lined the penitent forms, but also the details of their spiritual condition and family affairs and circumstances. To recall a hundred names caused him no embarrassment. He recollected the name of every convert, and every utterance of each one. 'So He giveth to His beloved in their sleep.' This astonishing endowment of memory was revoked as suddenly and unexpectedly as it was conferred. One night, in less than two years' time, he went to sleep in possession of it, and when he awoke—it was gone!"

Their labours together

The prayer meetings now became the scene of some remarkable happenings: the older members were awakened, and many restored to fellowship who had fallen away. Humphrey Jones and David Morgan would address the congregation and receive those who came forward to make a profession of faith. The number of these increased as time went on, and in spite of fears that the young, zealous converts would soon fall away, they continued, together with the older Christians, to serve God and His Church. Here is a description of the prayer meetings at that time.

"In the united services, the power of the Holy Spirit was being felt with gradually increasing intensity. It was in its terrors that the eternal became a reality to them first. They seemed plunged into depths of godly sorrow . . . For some weeks it was the voice of weeping and the sound of mourning that was heard in the meetings. The house was often so full of the divine presence that ungodly men trembled terror-stricken; and at the close, sometimes they fled as from some impending peril; at other times sat glued to their seats, ashamed and afraid to pass out in the presence of the church. Some, in their agitation, would leave their hats behind; and this ere long came to be interpreted as an indication that their owners would be the converts of the next service. After finding their way out, they would return, fascinated, in knots to the doors and windows, pushing them slightly ajar to get another glimpse of the strange scene that they had quitted. When the church members at last came out, like guilty creatures they would all retreat into the shadows, excepting some who would be too sorely wounded to flee."

In this way the revivalists began their work together, and they continued to labour at Ysbyty for some weeks, meeting with considerable success. One estimate is that, after two months of their work at Ysbyty and Pont-rhyd-y-groes, over 200 had been converted, while other estimates quote this figure as being the successes of the last three months of 1858 in those places.

The revival affected a nearby lead-mine in a remarkable way. "Many prayer meetings were held underground at Frongoch Mine. Not an oath was heard within the confines of the mine. At the name of Jesus every knee bowed of 'things under the earth'. One morning a prayer meeting was commenced as usual on reaching their work at six. Heaven penetrated into the pit and earth was forgotten. When the worshippers awoke from that sacred trance, they found it was two o'clock in the afternoon."

The prayer meetings at Ysbyty were terminated some time during December 1858, in order to consolidate and establish the converts, but a month later they were restarted as being very necessary in the face of continued conversions.

During October, David Morgan preached with new power in various churches in Cardiganshire. On the 17th of that month, he was at Pen-uwch, and his text was Philippians 3: 10, "That I may know him, and the power of his resurrection, and the fellowship of his sufferings, being made conformable unto his death". He spoke much about Humphrey Jones and the work at Pont-rhyd-y-groes. The following Sunday he was at Blaen-plwyf, and the last Sunday in October, he preached at the Tabernacl, Aberystwyth, on Psalm 126: 1-3, "When the Lord turned again the captivity of Zion, we were like them that dream. Then was our mouth filled with laughter, and our tongue with singing: then said they among the heathen, The Lord hath done great things for them. The Lord hath done great things for us; whereof we are glad". According to one testimony, he preached "with uncommon unction". When he preached in neighbouring churches on

the first two Sundays in November, his congregations noticed
the remarkable change which had come over his ministry and
desired him to continue with them. This he refused to do,
and called upon them to pray for a mighty visitation of the
Holy Spirit in their midst. On the second of these Sundays,
however, "a foul-mouthed youth was converted, and his lips
touched with a live coal from the altar. All his people were
practically heathen, and the lad immediately began work as a
home missionary. He besought his elder brother to attend
the house of God, and he for the sake of peace gave the
missionary a severe thrashing. The old folks were moved
with compassion towards the boy thus persecuted for
righteousness' sake; and as ointment upon his wounds, they
consoled him with the promise that they would accompany
him to the next religious service at the chapel. They went,
and the Lord laid His hand upon them both. The old man
had been fiery in temper and foul in speech in the past, but
the grace of God enabled him to fight a good fight against his
easily besetting sin. Sometimes, when irritated in the fields,
an oath would escape his lips almost unawares to him.
Immediately he would take in hand the work of self-discipline.
In his efforts to quell his passionate moods, the turf beneath
his feet would be stamped red; but he would not depart from
the spot, except as victor over himself. On such an occasion
he was heard to say to himself with a sigh, 'Ah! the *old*
sparks! the *old* sparks!'."

Humphrey Jones visited Llanafan early in November,
together with David Morgan, the latter taking little part in the
service; but the ground was hard and unprepared. On Wednesday, November 17th, the two revivalists visited Pontrhydfendigaid, where the church was in a deep slumber, and the
unconverted were shameless in their drunkenness, blasphemy
and profanation of the Sabbath. Morgan preached on Habak-
kuk 2: 4, "the just shall live by his faith", after which he

addressed the church meeting on the perils of self-righteous-ness. The following Sunday he preached at Lampeter, the text being Hosea 7: 9, "Strangers have devoured his strength, and he knoweth it not: yea, gray hairs are here and there upon him, yet he knoweth not", and this sermon was particu-larly blessed of God during the revival.

From Pontrhydfendigaid, the two men went to Tregaron, where they held a series of meetings, commencing on the Monday night of November 22nd. Hardly any movement was felt that first night, but on the Tuesday night it was apparent to all that the Spirit's powerful influences were being felt by many present. Morgan led the opening devotions under intense feelings, and continued under difficulty, but Jones was a disappointment to at least some of the congrega-tion, who had come from Llanddewibrefi to hear the revivalist. Wednesday, November 24th, at Tregaron was given to preach-ing, David Morgan's message in the morning being based upon Revelation 2: 4, "Nevertheless I have somewhat against thee, because thou hast left thy first love". In his prayer before Jones' sermon in the evening, Morgan cried out:

"We thank Thee, O Lord, that there are indications of a rising cloud. It is but a little one, like a man's hand, but it is a *cloud,* and it arises from the *sea.* Let the whole sky grow black! *Let the whole sky grow black! LET THE WHOLE SKY GROW BLACK!"*

Humphrey Jones preached with unction and great earnest-ness, and Morgan broke forth afresh into prayer before the final hymn was sung. This hymn was repeated several times over, and soon many of the older ones in the congregation were praising God, dancing as though filled with new wine, and crying out in great jubilation.

At Blaenpennal the next morning the two revivalists found "a prepared people, and the service was a memorable one".

Neither of them could minister because of the profuse weeping which overpowered the congregation, and Morgan could only cry out, his countenance transfigured as though seeing heaven opened, "Oh, the divine shekinah!" There were nine professions of conversion that morning, and the good work thus begun at Blaenpennal continued unabated for many months. Outbursts of praising and rejoicing were first heard at Blaenpennal in March 1859, and these continued during a period of some ten months. David Morgan visited Blaenpennal again, twice in January and once in February 1859. During the singing of a hymn after a sermon by Griffith Davies, on the night of December 4th 1859, there was a general acclamation and jubilation in the contemplation of the redemptive work of Christ. Even in June 1860, powerful influences were felt at a prayer meeting, and at the preaching services which followed.

On the afternoon of November 25th the two men preached at Llwynpiod, but the full impact of the revival was not felt here until early in 1859. At Swyddffynnon that evening Jones asked the elders to pray before he preached (on Amos 6: 1), but he felt that the hardness of the hearers was incompatible with a successful ministry, and requested the elders to pray again. Not until they had obeyed did he continue, and Morgan then followed, preaching on Hosea 7: 9. J. J. Morgan says that "Over 200 converts were received into this little village church", but the influx of converts did not begin until the first week in February 1859.

Under the blessing of God, the revivalists had together started a work, soon to spread throughout the land, news of which was already creating a stir amongst the churches. They had laboured together in Cardiganshire with no mean success, and had been instrumental in quickening God's people and in bringing many to a saving knowledge of Christ. In the December of 1858, however, they parted amicably, having agreed to work separately for the same end of reviving the church and converting the ungodly.

Their labours apart

Before going to Aberystwyth on December 19th, Humphrey Jones had held revival meetings alternately at Cnwch-coch and Cynon, and had seen much fruit to his labours. Such incessant labours, "in journeyings often . . . in weariness and painfulness, in watchings often" (2 Corinthians 11: 26, 27), together with the severe draining of nervous energy because of frequent preaching, could hardly be without their effect upon his mind and body, especially in the light of his weak condition when he arrived at Liverpool.

When he commenced the work at Aberystwyth in the December of 1858, he fervently desired that it should be a deeper and greater work than ever before. Queen Street Wesleyan church was, however, as cold and lifeless spiritually as the other country chapels he had already visited—and revived. For some reason the apathetic and spiritually stagnant condition of the Queen Street church became such an obsession to his mind as to make him alter his methods radically. These soon displayed certain irregularities, and were later to become altogether detrimental to the success of the revival. As a result of his changed views regarding the mode of promoting a revival, he refused to allow preaching and singing, and directed that the mission should be conducted as prayer meetings, together with the reading of God's Word. Another consequence of his obsession about the low condition of the church was his refusal to accept any into membership, although under the deepest spiritual convictions and manifestly partakers of saving grace. The unprepared condition of the church, in his opinion was totally inconducive to the Spirit's work in revival and his concern took on the nature of a mental distraction, giving rise to the irregularities already noted.

During the early months of 1859, conditions at Aberystwyth gradually deteriorated, and it was apparent that Humphrey Jones' mission, instead of proving the unparalleled success it was meant to be, was on the decline. Consequently, his mental distraction, which had governed his principles of procedure in the mission, became a mental aberration, which seriously altered his theological principles relating to divine revelation. The result was disastrous to him and to the mission. He kept very much to himself and maintained that he was the recipient of divine "revelations" which, delivered to the church, became "prophesyings". The culmination of this tragic mental process was a total departure from the authoritative Word of God, and the announcement of a "prophecy" to the effect that the Holy Spirit would descend in bodily form at Aberystwyth on a given date and at a given time, this event initiating the "millennium".

Humphrey Jones' remorse after the painful incident which ensued, when his error and failure were brought into sharp focus before a large gathering, knew no bounds, and he desired only oblivion and solitude. The Reverend Thomas Phillips visited Cardiganshire on behalf of the Bible Society in March 1860, and he records his impressions, making this statement:

"I was sorry to find that Mr. Humphrey Jones who was made so useful at the commencement, had been laid aside from public work . . . At present he takes no part in the services of the chapel of his own denomination . . . though urged to do so. It is said that he spends much time in private prayer, and professes to be too much *straitened* to engage in any public exercise, whether prayer or preaching; but still entertains the hope, if he does not fully believe, that he will yet be made useful to his countrymen."

After about four years he was enabled to preach with the Wesleyans in the Aberystwyth circuit, but early in 1869 it was necessary for him to have medical treatment. In 1871 he departed for America, where he laboured, with intermittent periods of ill-health, until his death at Chilton, Wisconsin, in 1895.

During December, David Morgan seems to have confined his labours to Cardiganshire, visiting some places, such as Bronnant, Pen-uwch and Pen-llwyn, twice before the end of 1858. As an indication of the difficulties he occasionally experienced, it is recorded that the only two converts at Bronnant were an Irishman and his wife, whose knowledge of Welsh was very scanty. When he revisited the village on December 29th, however, there were indications of a powerful movement of the Spirit, for as "the converts moved forward, some infinite power fell upon the audience, darting around like wildfire". The following anecdote is told of one of his visits to Pen-uwch.

"Are you coming to the prayer meeting?" said he to an old man working by the roadside. "No, not I," snorted the stone-breaker. "Come! come!" "I will *not* come to your prayer meeting. I can't understand how you chapel people find time to attend so many meetings. *I* can't afford to lose my work." "What would your loss amount to if you came?" "If I gave an hour I'd lose sixpence." "Well, here is a six-penny-bit for you; come to the service." "I don't want your sixpence or your service," was the irascible response. "Well, I must pray for you," said David Morgan. "You have a soul worth more than the world, in danger of eternal death." He knelt on the heap of stones, and pleaded with God to melt the stony-hearted old rebel. "Stop! *Stop!* I'll come with you," cried the veteran, grasping the minister by the arm. "What is it you want?" said David Morgan to him in the after-meeting. "Mercy for my poor soul," he replied. "I have grown too old for Victoria" (he was a discharged old soldier), "but perhaps Jesus Christ will enrol me in His army, and succour my poor soul."

His Sunday ministry at Pen-llwyn on December 12th was in many ways a preparation for greater things to come, for when he returned to the village on the 23rd of the same month, his preaching was eminently used to the eternal benefit of many, and the revival fire, thus kindled, blazed in the locality for several weeks. His son relates an incident which occurred during the sermon that night.

"In the middle of his sermon he startled his audience by suddenly exclaiming, 'If any of you here tonight deny the deity of the Son, I have nothing better to tell you than what Morgan Howell, Newport, shouted on Lampeter bridge, "Though he was rich, yet for our sakes He became poor. He became poor when He came to Bethlehem; tell me, when was He rich?"' This remark was utterly irrelevant to the preacher's subject-matter, and no one could conjecture whence it came, and whither it went. The mystery was solved in the after-meeting, for among the converts were three Unitarians . . . whose presence in the service was quite accidental, and certainly unknown to the preacher."

The writer also records that, for many weeks after this remarkable meeting, when the crowds went home from the services at the chapel, nothing would be heard but the sound of praise and jubilation.

Thomas Edwards of Pen-llwyn

Further, it was also the night when Thomas Edwards "received that baptism of fire that made him henceforth an apostle of zeal and power". As a result, when he wrote to the *Drysorfa* towards the end of February 1859, giving expression to his fears and prejudices regarding the work, he was able to add that they had been wholly swept away.

"We have our fears lest the work should prove superficial, and that we are bringing men into the visible Church of Christ who have not been convinced of sin, and converted by the Spirit of God. Most of us, however, have lost those fears, and we cannot avoid coming to the conclusion that God is at work, saving the souls of men."

By the time Thomas Edwards wrote that article, he himself had laboured in many places as another of the "men of vision", and since the middle of February, he had been with David Morgan holding revival meetings at Aberystwyth. His own ministry at Pen-llwyn was blessed at that time, the chapel being filled to capacity, and the congregation deriving greater blessings from his ministry than that of any other. Occasionally he was called upon to be the vanguard of the revival in places exceptionally hardened and opposed to revival, as for example, Cwmystwyth. On many occasions he accompanied David Morgan in the work, his opinion of the revivalist being such that he is reported to have said: "I am willing to chop the wood and draw the water for David Morgan. I thank God daily for raising him up to do so much work, and I count it a privilege that I am allowed to say a word with a preacher who moves congregations as the rushes."

Evan Phillips

Thomas Edwards was not the only one who had the privilege of working with David Morgan during the revival. Evan Phillips, who was ordained in 1860 as minister of the Calvinistic Methodist church at Newcastle Emlyn, accompanied Morgan on his journey in North Wales during June 1859. It was while he was preaching at Blaenpennal that Evan Phillips was first stirred by the powerful influences of the Spirit in revival. While he was delivering his sermon, the praise and rejoicing of the congregation were so great that he was unable to draw his remarks to a conclusion. He was again stirred at the remarkable session of the Cardiganshire Presbytery which was held at Aberaeron on February 9th and 10th, 1859, and which proved to be the vital turning point for many of the elders and ministers present, in favour of David Morgan and the revival.

By the end of 1858 many of the churches in Cardiganshire had been awakened and the number of converts added to them was quite considerable. Already some of the characteristics of the revival were being clearly defined, and its leading instruments were being abundantly used, and becoming more and more prominent. The preaching of the Word was being honoured, and the usefulness of the prayer meetings was being amply demonstrated. The society or church meeting at the close of the preaching service was fulfilling its purpose under the effective guidance of the revivalists, and their itinerant ministry was chiefly instrumental in the spreading of the flame.

In places further afield news of the Cardiganshire work served as added fuel to a fire already kindled by reports of the American work, and the united prayer meetings called to pray for a similar outpouring were to prove eminently successful. The infusion of new life, already begun in the churches of Cardiganshire, was to spread gradually as an unquenchable conflagration, and under the divine blessing it was to engulf almost the whole of the Principality. There were many difficulties to be overcome, and many foes to be conquered, but the work was soon to establish itself as being truly of God, and therefore the prosperity of this remarkable movement of the Holy Spirit was ensured.

4. THE COURSE OF EVENTS

1859 was to prove a momentous year for the Welsh Nonconformist churches. In the beginning of that year there were clear indications of increasing spiritual activity in their midst, particularly in the prayer meetings. Cardiganshire had already received untold and uncommon blessings, but even these were to be eclipsed by the astonishing experiences and incalculable benefits of the coming months. The morals of whole communities were vastly improved, and in some localities there were but few who made no profession of a vital and saving Christianity.

During the year the quickening of the Church was to evidence itself in more powerful, authoritative preaching, and in more effectual, fervent praying; the Bible came to be more widely read, and family worship received new life and impetus. Each of the Nonconformist denominations felt the impact of the revival, but principally the Calvinistic Methodists and the Congregationalists, even as their ministers were the most prominent in promoting the revival, and more widely used at that time. The Established church was slow to accept the necessity and authenticity of the work, but where there were sympathetic clergy and godly laymen, the revival was none the less successful than amongst the Nonconformists. It was inevitable that those counties adjoining Cardiganshire should be the next to prove the full blessing of the revival, and in Carmarthen, Merioneth and Montgomery, the work was especially thorough and effective. From these counties, the wave of revival radiated to the remainder, until, by the spring of 1860, every county in the Principality had felt its effects.

The end of 1858

A number of churches had set themselves to pray for revival before the end of 1858, or early in 1859, and these waited expectantly to receive the gracious visitation of the Holy Spirit in their midst. In the main, prayer meetings were commenced through hearing of the work in America and Cardiganshire, and such a situation obtained at Llandudno, Waunfawr near Caernarvon, Blaenau Ffestiniog, Pennal, Ystradfellte and a host of other places. There were a number of causes for these otherwise isolated cases of preparation for the revival, but generally the procedure was governed by local conditions, and sometimes incidents, which acted as a stimulus to the churches, and motivated the commencement of prayer meetings to seek revival.

Since 1855, a flourishing slate-quarrying industry had brought a substantial increase in the population of Pentredŵr near Llangollen, but this material prosperity was seriously detrimental to the morals of the community, and it became proverbial for its drunkenness and profanity. The Calvinistic Methodist church became alarmed at this prolific and cancerous growth of ungodliness, and was resolved to make the church and the locality a matter of earnest prayer to God. A weekly prayer meeting was commenced in the summer of 1858 with the express purpose of seeking God's face for a mighty awakening. At the beginning of 1859 the Wesleyans joined with them and the prayer meetings were held each night of the week. These flourished, as was evident in the growth of the numbers which attended, in the earnestness of the prayers, and in the confidence in God's faithfulness to His promises. They continued for some three weeks without any unusual occurrences, and were followed by a series of preaching services. On Thursday night, January 27th, while a Wesleyan minister, William Morgan, was preaching on Matthew 16: 26, "For what is a man profited if he shall gain the whole world, and lose his own soul?", showing vividly the dangerous consequences of losing the soul, the cloud burst upon them, and issued in a period of torrential showers of the divine favour. By April 1859, seventy had been added to the Calvinistic Methodist church alone.

The sudden death of a young man, under conviction of sin after hearing a solemnising sermon, considerably disturbed the Cwmtirmynach locality, Merionethshire, in the October of 1858. Many were converted under the ordinary means of grace during the weeks which followed, so that, when David Morgan and Evan Phillips visited there on June 28th, 1859, some forty had already been accepted into membership.

At Maethlon, near Towyn, the number of members at the Calvinistic Methodist church was eight just before the revival, and the locality was hardened in sin and indifferent to eternal issues. By the beginning of winter, 1858, however, they were moved to pray for revival on hearing of the success of the gospel in Cardiganshire through the testimony of one in their midst who had been there. The Friday night prayer meetings, thus started, increased in number, and a general feeling of soberness and concern for spiritual things was felt in the neighbourhood. The powerful, divine influences descended in a Sunday morning prayer meeting, held before the preaching service, when many were dissolved into tears, overcome by the weight of their convictions and feelings. The Reverend Robert Williams of Aberdovey heard the cries as he approached the chapel, and he felt his own frame as though electrified by the spiritual energies. That Sunday's ministry proved fruitful, and there were conversions every week in their midst for a considerable time. Robert Williams returned to Aberdovey determined that his flock should be brought to a similar place of blessing, and David Morgan could write in his diary for March 24th, 1859, that sixty-one had already been converted there. Similar times of refreshing were being experienced at Barmouth, and during the three months up to May 21st, 1859, seventy conversions had been recorded.

Meanwhile, similar things were happening in Montgomeryshire. At Meifod, for example, Evan Davies, the minister of the Wesleyan chapel, had been zealous for the revival since his induction to the charge in August 1858. A mission held by the Wesleyans in October 1858, was greatly blessed, and thirteen were added to the church. The Calvinistic Methodists joined with the Wesleyans before the end of the year, when their suspicions regarding the work had been resolved, and the united prayer meetings were soon well-attended and proved profitable. Simultaneously, at Llangurig, there was better attendance at the means of grace, and a prayer meeting was started, meeting twice a week, in February 1859. About forty were added to the church, which in 1858 numbered twenty-four members, and by May 1860, there were also about thirty young people being prepared for membership in the church.

The New Year, 1859

David Morgan, however, confined his labours to Cardiganshire during January and February. Perhaps it could be said that the evening service at Devil's Bridge on New Year's Day set the whole tone of the year's labours. An old minister wrote of that service:

"The evening service was terrible. So near was the revivalist to his God, that his face shone like that of an angel, so that none could gaze steadfastly at him. Many of the hearers swooned. On the way home I dared not break the silence for miles. Towards midnight I ventured to say, 'Didn't we have blessed meetings, Mr. Morgan?' 'Yes,' he replied; and after a pause, added, 'The Lord would give us great things, if He could only trust us'. 'What do you mean?' I asked. 'If He could trust us not to steal the glory for ourselves.' Then the midnight air rang with his cry, at the top of his voice, 'Not unto us, O Lord, not unto us, but unto *Thy* name give glory'."

David Morgan visited several places for the second time during January, and he had amazing power while ministering at Graig, Aber-ffrwd and Llangwyryfon. "Stalwart fellows from the mountains would moan as if crushed beneath stupendous burdens or pierced with swords. Some would weep as if their hearts were breaking, others fall into ecstatic swoons. Waves of power often overwhelmed them, and most extraordinary physical effects accompanied their impact. Many leaped and danced in the exuberance of their rapture. The Lord made their feet literally like hinds' feet, and made them walk upon their high places. When the breeze blew strong from the eternal hills, the established formalities and proprieties of a religious service were cast to the winds; all the Lord's people became prophets, and the ordinary barriers of diffidence and reticence having been swept away, began to speak, sing or pray as the Spirit gave them utterance."

Morgan was accompanied by Thomas Edwards when he visited New Quay, Penmorfa, Aberaeron and Ffos-y-ffin, where the preaching was drowned in the praising, and all present wept without shame or restraint. Three events took place in January which were of importance to David Morgan; the Cardiganshire presbytery at Blaenannerch, his visit to Rhydyfelin and the Borth preaching festival. At the first of these, it was obvious that the elders and members at Blaenannerch were eagerly awaiting the revivalist and his message, while the officials of the Presbytery were cold and suspicious in their attitude. The minister at Blaenannerch, John Jones, probably expressed the fears and opinions of many of his brethren in disputation with David Morgan.

" 'What is this that I hear about you, David, my boy?' said John Jones. 'What have you heard?', asked David Morgan guardedly. 'What have I heard? What means this lugging of people into church fellowship without giving them time to sit down and consider and count the cost before they begin to build?' 'What time ought a sinner to get to consider, Mr. Jones?' 'More than you give them, by all accounts.' 'You are criticising my method; what is your idea of a reasonable period for considering this great question?' Accepting the challenge, John Jones retorted, 'A month is not too much, at least.' David Morgan saw that his enemy was delivered into his hand, and replied, 'Well! Well! God's Spirit says, Today; the devil says, Tomorrow; but the old evangelist of Blaenannerch says, A month hence will do'."

Thomas Edwards and David Morgan preached in the evening service, and there were great cries during the meeting, but neither the accounts of the work, nor the impression created by the two revivalists were to the satisfaction of the officers of the Presbytery, although most of the representatives were sympathetic. The church at Blaenannerch, however, could trace the blessings of revival back to the labours of Thomas Edwards and David Morgan that day, so that six weeks later sixty had been converted in their midst, apart from twenty-eight of their young people who had been accepted into full membership. News of David Morgan's proposed visit to Rhydyfelin had reached certain of the more sceptical ministers and laymen in and around Aberystwyth, and they resolved to investigate the rumours concerning the upstart-revivalist.

"The meeting had begun before they arrived; and as they stood in the lobby, they could hear the preacher's voice, and it pierced each heart like a knife. 'They were conquered before they saw his face, and henceforward he was to them as an angel of God'."

By February 21st, 104 had been added to the church. Robert Roberts and John Lewis, two Calvinistic Methodist ministers, preached on the first day of the Borth preaching festival. On the following day, Thomas Edwards and David Morgan were to minister, but while journeying to their destination they heard that Robert Roberts was antagonistic to the revival. Upon hearing this they spent some time in prayer, and their preaching during the day was accompanied by unusual power and success. David Morgan recorded in his diary: "As the converts stood up to come forward, some divine power fell on the hearts of scores, and many burst out crying for their lives; that is, some of the old members, not the converts. These were weeping and trembling." By these means the suspicion and prejudice of many were to be overcome, and before the end of February the majority of the ministers and elders of Cardiganshire were to stand uncompromisingly by the side of David Morgan and the revival.

February, 1859

The turning point in this connection was undoubtedly the presbytery held at Aberaeron in early February. The churches had been urged to pray since the previous presbytery for God's blessing on the deliberations at Aberaeron. The Tabernacl church there, at least, had responded by holding a prayer meeting each Sunday at 8.30 a.m. A number of revival addresses were given at the first evening's service, and a witness describes the meeting as "one that would not be forgotten for all eternity by any living who was present". The same witness referred to the presbytery as "the most amazing ever seen by any living person". Evan Phillips, who was present, wrote his reminiscences of the meetings to the *Goleuad* of May 5th, 1905.

"The group acknowledged as leaders in the monthly meeting were antagonistic, and even menacing. It seems that they had come there with fists clenched and teeth set, and their new ropes ready to bind the half-crazy preacher, as they esteemed him. They thought they were doing God service. Many, therefore, had anxious forebodings as to the revivalist's fate. By the evening service, it was clear that he needed no earthly champion. God's presence filled the place. Those good brethren who had proposed to defend the ark had vanished already. The intense glow pervading the place vindicated itself as God's fire."

David Morgan preached three times during the festival, and he did so with power and conviction, the second afternoon's service being abundantly blessed. Evan Phillips remembered the following scene:

"The revivalist stood in the pulpit and glanced around the audience, gazing more especially at the crowd of young people in the gallery. That gaze was terrible. Hardly any one in the gallery could endure it. With one impulse they bent their heads like a sensitive plant touched. 'The world's sin is great,' he says. The words fall like lead on the hearts of the multitude. 'Christ's atonement is greater,' he adds; and a shower of tears falls through a bright sky of joy."

By the end of the week following the presbytery meetings, forty had sought admittance to the church, and it was evident that the work thus begun had gone on from strength to strength, for by 1860 about 200 had been added. The change effected by the revival in the religious sphere at Aberaeron was as revolutionary as it was beneficial.

"So far as the *externals* of religion are concerned, they were never in a more prosperous state than before the dawning

of this revival.   But, as for the *internals*—the spiritual temple
—these were far from being in a satisfactory condition . . . A
happy change is everywhere observed—our prayer meetings
are become crowded, and a powerful spirit of prayer has laid
hold of the churches . . . One of the most striking characteristics of this movement is its effects on young people, and
even on children . . . The youth of our congregations are
nearly all the subjects of deep religious impressions . . . Very
young people, yea, children from ten to fourteen years of age,
gather together to hold prayer meetings, and pray very fervently . . . We have never seen such an outburst of feeling
as . . . in many that have recently been brought under
religious impressions . . . Some, after sustaining a severe
struggle with their heart-convictions for many days and nights
without sleep and without rest, happily at last find peace in
Christ to their weary souls, and resolve henceforth to live in
Christ and to Him."

The Aberaeron presbytery therefore served a dual purpose: it opened the flood-gate of the revival to the southern
parts of the county, especially amongst the Calvinistic
Methodists; and it was also instrumental, under the inspired
guidance of such men as David Morgan, Thomas Edwards
and Morgan James, in removing the prejudice and hostility in
the minds of many ministers and laymen.

David Morgan continued his tremendous task of reviving
the churches of Cardiganshire during February, venturing
south into Carmarthenshire only at the end of the month.   He
began the month at Llanilar, which he had previously visited
on December 31st, 1858; each time the chapel had been filled
with eager, expectant congregations, and the ministry had
been powerful and successful.   Twenty were converted on the
first occasion, thirty-six on the second occasion, and by the end
of February there had been 147 recorded conversions.

According to his custom the revivalist prayed for people by name, and at Llanilar there was at least one of the local gentry who objected to being included in his intercessions: "Who is David Morgan, Ysbyty", he roared, "that he should take liberties with my name? When I next see him, I'll teach that malapert a lesson." He was shooting in a cover by the roadside a few days afterwards, when his servant said to him, "There comes David Morgan!" The squire stalked to the hedge with a scowling countenance. While the revivalist was far distant, the affronted gentleman stood with menacing brow, but as the rider drew near the great man began to bend at the knees, and as he approached he crouched lower and lower, until he was completely hidden from sight when the preacher came opposite. "I couldn't say a word to him," said the squire to his man. "His countenance was different from usual today."

A week later David Morgan came again to Llanilar. On the way he frequently deserted his companion, retiring for private prayer when a gap in the hedge gave him an opportunity. "We shall have a wonderful meeting tonight," he averred; "many will be saved tonight." This presentiment was verified, for fifty-one sought salvation. Among them was a man by the name of Taylor, a gardener at Castle-on-Hill. He was practically a heathen, though he sometimes attended the parish church. He was swept into the Nonconformist service by the flood of the revivalist's popularity, and the light of life dawned upon the darkness of his heart.

Whenever David Morgan gave the right hand of fellowship to a man who was the head of a household, he urged and insisted that he should forthwith begin to conduct family worship. Taylor shrank from this heavy yoke, until he remembered that he had at home a copy of the Book of Common Prayer. His wife, rejoicing that her partner was no longer an enemy to her Saviour, placed the big Bible on the little round table after supper, and she was astonished by her husband's unfaltering approach to it. She little guessed that he had already secretly secured the Prayer Book, and having found an appropriate collect, had turned the leaf down and hid the book in his pocket. He calmly drew the Bible to him, and having opened the book, he found the place where was written the story of Christ's last hours in Gethsemane. As he read his heart melted within him; there distilled upon his soul an unction from the Holy One, and unbidden tears glistened ere they fell on the sacred page. When he closed the Book there was a lump in his throat; he fell on his knees, and poured forth his soul in strains of penitence and praise. Then he retired upstairs, musing abstractedly and sweetly on what God had wrought within him, and it was only when he felt the volume in his pocket as he undressed that he first remembered the provision he had made for facing the ordeal of family prayer. When this incident was related shortly afterwards to the eminent preacher, John Jones, Blaenannerch, he enjoyed the recital hugely. "Do you see the secret?" he cried. "If he wanted formalism, he should have avoided Gethsemane; *he went too near the Blood.*"

David Morgan's endeavours to stir the churches were not always unopposed, and at Lledrod one influential elder embittered his fellow-members against the revivalist's work. Two of the remaining elders had heard David Morgan at Llanilar, and had requested him to visit their church, which he did. In spite of a cold reception, at any rate in the number present, his preaching was attended with power and eight were converted. A few days later, on a second visit, forty-seven sought refuge in Christ, many of them famed for their iniquity and ungodliness.

Llangeitho and Aberystwyth were probably the two most important places visited by David Morgan in February. Before his visit to Llangeitho on Thursday, February 24th, the church's lukewarmness and apathy had been challenged by three Cardiganshire ministers, Thomas Edwards (Cwmystwyth), Daniel Evans (Ffos-y-ffin) and Morgan James. Daniel Evans had spoken of the amazing scenes witnessed during and after the Aberaeron presbytery, and as a result two had remained for the "society" meeting. On Monday night, February 21st, eight had sought admission to church membership, and when Morgan James preached on the following Wednesday night, nineteen were converted. According to David Morgan's diary, sixty-nine had already been converted at Llangeitho before his first visit. He records that the meeting at Llangeitho was an "extraordinary" one, and that forty-one remained for the "society". Greater things were to come, for by August 1859, a correspondent of *Y Cyfaill o'r Hen Wlad* could report:

"We have had experience at Llangeitho of four revivals within a period of fifty years, but this is the most powerful. Dozens of old folk who had stubbornly resisted all these revivals have been forced to bend now. We have received three hundred new members within the first five months of this year."

In the fifteen days before David Morgan's visit to Aberystwyth on Friday, February 11th, in company with Thomas Edwards, 151 had been converted in the town. When both had preached that night sixty made profession of conversion, after an initial pause, as though they were being held back. On a sudden impulse, it was decided to hold a prayer meeting on the Saturday afternoon, and although there was no public announcement, Tabernacl chapel, which held 1,200 people, was full. A further thirty-six were converted, and by the end of March, about 400 members had been added to the church. Two of these were notorious for their riotous living:

"While Captain Williams of the *Peggy* was praying one evening in a service in a schoolroom, one of the vilest reprobates of the town rushed in under the influence of drink. The reverent solemnity pervading the meeting checked his roistering insolence. He listened and scanned the scene for a few minutes, then suddenly dropped on his knees, shouting with an exceeding bitter cry, 'O God, be merciful unto Dave the bully!' Then he moved to the front, mingling his supplications with those of the captain, and making his wife the subject of his prayers. 'Betty is in the house, Thou knowest, O Lord; go there, Lord, and if the door is locked, unship it off the hinges, and save Betty, Lord!'. In a short time, Betty too came in with a wild look, and cried immediately, 'Lord, have mercy on me, the biggest sinner in Trefechan'. Their reformation was lasting."

The Established church could also report a substantial increase, for by February 1860, 260 new members had been received at Aberystwyth and Llanbadarn. By the beginning of March, David Morgan had moved into Carmarthenshire, having commenced his itinerary at Newcastle Emlyn.

Until about the end of February 1859, the revival had been very closely associated with Humphrey Jones and David Morgan. They had confined their labours to Cardiganshire, and they had experienced in a very real way the tremendous energies of the eternal Spirit. The powerful workings of the Holy Spirit had in a sense been concentrated geographically, and for that reason, the revival had been equated with their field of service.

As news of the work spread, and as others were being used in their own spheres, however, it was no longer possible —or at least, it was not longer accurate—to equate the revival with the preaching engagements of David Morgan. There were three main indications of this. In the first place, within the territory covered by the Cardiganshire presbytery, more and more ministers and preachers were bearing the torch of revival, in the churches of their own charge, and also by means of their itinerant ministries. These included Morgan James, Daniel Evans, Evan Phillips and David Morgans, to mention only a few. Secondly, outside this region, and coming more and more into prominence during the spring months of 1859, were men of differing denominations, but baptised with the same fire, and reaping the same harvest from their inspired preaching. Thirdly, ever-multiplying prayer meetings were being started in an increasing number of places. These had been stimulated into existence by news of the Cardiganshire work and were impelled forward by the transfusion of its appeal and success. Under such influences, and in such places, the work of the revival showed a vigorous growth and spread with rapidly-increasing momentum.

During February some of the most amazing scenes of the revival were witnessed in places as far apart as Tregaron, Machynlleth and Llanharan. They were symptomatic of an intensifying of the power and effect of the revival, and also of the widening of its scope and influence. D. Davies described in 1905 what he termed as a "meeting which profoundly changed the character of the revival", and which took place in a school-room outside Tregaron on February 17th, 1859.

"A general jubilation broke out in that meeting, in which almost all the young people present joined, as well as the old. The following night similar meetings took place at Blaenpennal; and by the Sunday night, Llangeitho, Llwynpiod, Llanddewibrefi and Rhydfendigaid were on fire. That was the beginning of the great outburst of jubilation in the revival. The great deluge of converts into the church could be dated from that time . . . all the religious means of grace, of all kinds, were subsequently under a most manifest anointing, especially the preaching."

The Sunday referred to above certainly proved to be a memorable one at Tregaron, under the ministry of David Morgans. While singing the hymn before the sermon in the morning service, scores of people, scattered in the congregation, gave vent to their feelings in loud cries. This continued for some two hours, and at the end thirty gave themselves to the Saviour. The evening service was even more remarkable, for with every sentence of the sermon a strong overpowering influence was felt, and the exultation of the congregation knew no bounds. Fifty-seven were accepted into the "society" at the close of the evening service.[3]

There were similarities in the pattern of events at Machynlleth. Early in February, six or seven people had attended a prayer meeting at the Calvinistic Methodist church during the week, and on the Saturday night they felt that divine, heavenly influences were at work in their midst. During the Sunday which followed, Robert Williams preached with exceptional power. In the evening service the congregation could not be restrained from breaking forth into exultation and praise. According to the testimony of William Griffiths, writing early in 1860, it was in February 1859 that his church had experiences comparable to those of Pentecost. As a result, he continues:

". . . anxious inquirers came forward in dozens, some under strong mental emotions, perceiving their lost state as sinners; and shortly they received relief to their minds by exercising faith in the merits of our Lord and Saviour Jesus Christ . . . The churches are generally doubled in number, and new inquirers are continually coming forward. The heavenly fire still continues to burn, and the flames have

[3] See Note, p. 121.

spread throughout the county at large. All religious denominations are cordially united in social prayer meetings, and
the descent of divine influence among us is evident."

During that year William Griffiths received more than 650
into membership at his church, and the experiences of the
beginning of 1860 were to parallel, if not to surpass, those
of February 1859.   Furthermore, in the months which followed, the revival spread rapidly in Glamorganshire, particularly through the Congregationalist Monthly Meetings, at
Hirwaun in March, Aberdare in April, Aberaman and
Mountain Ash in May.

March, 1859

In the same period of time, that is, between the spring
of 1859 and that of 1860, David Morgan toured extensively
throughout Wales.   On his itineraries he was occasionally
accompanied by a fellow-worker, and interspersed between
them he sometimes laboured for short periods in Cardiganshire.   During the early part of March he visited several
places in Carmarthenshire, and although his successes
did not equal those in Cardiganshire, they were none the less
substantial.   At Bethel (Baptist) chapel, Caeo, when he had
preached on Hosea 7: 9, his own impression was that it had
been "a very hard service".   The estimate of the minister of
the church was appreciably different.

"It was a remarkable service.   The appeals of the preacher
were extraordinarily powerful.   I was at Bethel next Sunday
morning, and forty penitents joined the church.   None of the
hearers who went out proceeded beyond the graveyard.   The
deacons went out among them urging them to surrender, and
forty more obeyed.   In my next service at Salem, the sister
church, thirty-nine joined!   They were baptised in the Ddol-
wen brook, and the first to be immersed was Dr. Timothy

Richards, China. These converts formed the strength of the church in ten years. I attribute this great upheaval to David Morgan's sermon on 'Ephraim's grey hairs'."

By March 17th, David Morgan was back again in Aberystwyth, and he remained in that part of Cardiganshire for the rest of the month. The following item appeared in *The Nonconformist* of March 1859:

"A valued correspondent informs us of a powerful awakening in the county of Cardigan, embracing also a considerable part of Carmarthenshire. The week-day and Sabbath-day services at churches and chapels were crowded. Hundreds are coming over to the Lord's side . . . a deep and genuine work of grace is going on. It is said that no less than 4,000 have already become decided in Cardiganshire alone, and the movement seems to be making rapid progress. There is no excitement; but a deep, silent, and awfully solemn impression prevails everywhere."

This report was, however, somewhat out-dated, because the revival had, by that time, touched places much further afield than envisaged by the "valued correspondent".

Thus, in the reports of the revival, given at the North Wales Association held at Holyhead in March, some of the brethren spoke of "movements", similar to those in Cardiganshire, already being experienced in parts of Merionethshire and Flintshire. The chief characteristics of the work were a spirit of prayer, followed by a delight in, and power attending, the ministry, together with considerable increases to the churches. Other matters relating to revival noted at the same session were: the possibility of erring, on the one hand by trying to create a revival ourselves, seeking thereby to imitate the Holy Spirit, without receiving Him, or even being prepared thereto; or erring on the other hand by being indifferent and careless, maintaining that the Spirit must do all, and that man is to do nothing; further, there was a duty laid upon all, but especially upon ministers and elders, of furthering the work of revival, and of building up the converts in the faith. The account concludes:

"Let us seek to pray that the awakening influences will go from strength to strength, until our churches in every town and locality have been quickened, increased, and uplifted to rejoice in the Lord. An intense conviction of the need for an awakening, earnest prayer for it, together with a humble and self-denying spirit in readiness to welcome it, through whatever instruments, and in whichever form it may come, are sure fore-runners of it."

In Merionethshire, the Calvinistic Methodist churches at Pennal and Penrhyndeudraeth were being awakened, the prayers of God's people becoming more fervent. Similar movements were being felt in Edeyrn, Jerusalem (Bethesda), and Pwllheli in Caernarvonshire. At Pwllheli, the church had been stirred before the visit of Robert Williams for the March preaching festival. Fifteen were added to the church at that time, and by the end of April, the number of converts had increased to over 100. The number of converts became fewer towards the end of May, but early in 1860 there was a second wave of blessing, and by June of that year there were nearly 400 converts. There were signs of an awakening at Pontrobert, and at Rhosllannerchrugog, where, after a week of prayer meetings, the Flintshire presbytery was abundantly blessed, and within a fortnight thirty-one were added to the church.

The prayer meetings of the Congregational cause at Abergwili, Carmarthenshire, were being well attended during March. The minister, D. C. Jones, had been disheartened because of difficulties, but was restrained from leaving the church on the appeal of the majority of the members. While preaching on Sunday night, March 27th, a deep impression was made upon all present, which produced much fruit. He later gave this account of the service:

"It was evident, from the earnest attention paid to the sermon and to every part of the service, that a deep feeling pervaded the congregation. I endeavoured to deepen and draw out this earnest feeling by preaching from Hosea 13: 13, ['The sorrows of a travailing woman shall come upon him: he is an unwise son: for he should not stay long in the place of the breaking forth of children'.] This was done in my two congregations and with marked effect. During the succeeding months I had the inexpressible pleasure of giving the right hand of fellowship to upwards of two hundred persons. I am thankful to say that, with few exceptions, they give one abundant satisfaction."

Already then, the revival had been felt in a wider field than was generally supposed or appreciated at the time. It by no means covered the counties mentioned thoroughly, or to the extent which it would eventually, but those isolated localities where the flame had been lit would soon be linked up as the intervening areas were engulfed in the fire.

April, 1859

David Morgan again confined his labours, in the main, to Cardiganshire during April, venturing only as far as Pennal on April 6th, where he had much succour in delivering his message, and much success following upon it. J. J. Morgan records that, at "the Monthly Meeting soon afterwards, the tide of joy ran so high that Robert Williams could not preach". He continues:

"The Venerable Richard Humphreys, Dyffryn, appealed for quietness. One of the firebrands of the revival volunteered his aid to achieve this end. 'I'll take care of this patch,' he said, 'and woe to the man who begins to disturb! Go on, Mr. Williams.' By frowning on one, and shaking a second, and threatening a third, he kept the most noisy in check, until the minister led his audience to gaze at Calvary; when, feeling his charge slipping from his grasp, he repudiated his self-imposed responsibility, addressing the preacher, 'Oh, well, if you are going that way, between you and them!' "

David Morgan also visited such places as Machynlleth, Pen-uwch, Llangwyryfon, and Llwynpiod, where the April presbytery was held. The topic under discussion was 'Prayer', and the Moderator criticised the new practice of praying for people by name. The atmosphere was cold and dismal until David Morgan was invited to speak, when the whole tenor of the meeting was changed to one of praise and gladness.

Various ministers visited Cil-y-cwm, Carmarthenshire, during 1859, and their ministries were richly blessed. The awakening began in April, when prayer meetings were commenced. These prospered and became more and more fruitful in the earnestness of the prayers, and also in the numbers of conversions. One report stated that there had been "a most powerful revival at Cil-y-cwm, and about two hundred souls" had been added to one church.

The Reverend John Phillips was mightily used at Llantrisant during the third week of April; while at Bala, Thomas Edwards was seeking to rouse the religious to a sense of responsibility. The students at Bala were already partakers of the blessing, and the nearby villages of Tal-y-bont and Llidiardau had also felt some movements, but Bala remained unmoved until David Morgan and Evan Phillips preached there on Sunday, June 26th.

Llanwrtyd first felt the impact of the revival under the ministry of Morris Morgan on April 17th. He had been to Tregaron and had experienced the power of the revival there. After his sermon on Daniel 2: 44, "And in the days of these kings shall the God of heaven set up a kingdom, which shall never be destroyed . . .", the whole congregation was fired with ecstasy and exultation. Many from Rhandir-mwyn, Carmarthenshire, took the revival blaze home with them. From Llanwrtyd the revival spread to Gorwydd and Llangamarch, and from Llangamarch to Merthyr Cynog. In this way, Llanwrtyd was of cardinal importance to the 1859 revival in Breconshire, the most powerful influences and the most glorious fruit being received as a result of that extraordinary service.

May-June, 1859

David Morgan spent the latter part of May and the beginning of June in Pembrokeshire. "At Fishguard, the herald of the revival was a storm of weeping which swept suddenly one evening over a children's meeting . . . It was at Trevine that the fires of the revival burnt most brightly in the whole of Pembrokeshire: 110 new members were added to one church in the village." The old as well as the young benefited from the revival, and many who had been deep in sin came to pray with great fluency and effectiveness.[4]

On his way to Merionethshire, David Morgan again returned to Cardiganshire in the early part of June. By June 14th he was at Dolgelley, accompanied by Evan Phillips, and the two laboured together in that county for some weeks, visiting such places as Barmouth, Penrhyndeudraeth, Llangwm, Dinmael and Bala.

Meanwhile, in other counties, the revival continued to spread. Morgan James was present at the Tredegar presbytery of June, and the fire started to burn brightly during the sessions of the presbytery. At Llanrwst, Denbighshire, a

[4] See Note, p. 121.

young people's prayer meeting was initiated in June; because of the lack of numbers, it soon became a united prayer meeting, the Nonconformist bodies joining together to pray for revival. Their prayers were answered, and the Holy Spirit came into their midst towards the end of July. At Trefriw and Betws-y-coed, Caernarvonshire, similar prayer meetings were commenced in the same month, but they did not experience the full tide of blessing until October. Robert Williams visited Tregeiriog, Denbighshire, about the middle of the summer, and two were added to the church as a first-fruit of what was to follow only in the early months of 1860.

The June issue of the *Drysorfa* gives a numerical estimate of the fruit of the revival in Cardiganshire, and reads as follows:

"The converts among the Calvinistic Methodists alone number above *eight thousand* . . . at Tabernacl, Aberystwyth, about 500; Rhydfendigaid about 400; Tregaron about 400; Rhiw-bwys, Llanrhystyd about 200; Lledrod about 200; and many other churches have received more than 200 additions."

Thomas Edwards and others gave an account of the progress of the revival at the North Wales Association held at Denbigh in June. Little notice seems to have been taken of the revival, except to point out the responsibility of all present "to use such a valuable season as a time of awakening to establish the Church in the faith and to cultivate her in Christian virtues".

Monmouthshire, however, seems to have benefited considerably from the Assembly of the Congregational churches held at Beaufort, at the end of June. "Preparatory prayer meetings had been held for seven weeks . . . the second day, (Dr.) John Thomas of Liverpool preached a magnificent sermon on the subject of 'revival' from Psalm 102: 13, 'Thou shalt arise, and have mercy upon Zion: for the time to favour her, yea, the set time, is come'." The minister of Beaufort, Thomas Rees, could report that between April 1859 and March 1860 "at least two thousand" had joined the Congregational churches of Monmouthshire.

The summer of 1859

Before the end of July the revival had spread to quite extensive areas in Monmouth, Glamorgan and Carmarthen. Cardiganshire was still experiencing great things, and David Morgan could write in his diary for July 20th, "Bronnant Monthly Meeting. A most remarkable meeting, great exultation during the two days". J. J. Morgan adds that there were 110 converts. A thanksgiving service for God's mercy in the revival was held on Fron-goch Hill, near Ysbyty Ystwyth, on July 12th, when there were 3,000 present.

Many places in Caernarvonshire experienced powerful movements on Sunday, August 21st. "On Monday morning the amazing news was blazed abroad that overpowering spiritual forces had descended the previous evening on every congregation in the neighbourhood." The effects at Llanddeiniolen continued unabated for some months, and were keenly felt, particularly among the young people, the prayer meetings being abundantly used as means of blessing. Over 100 had been added to the churches there and at Cefn-y-waun by January 1860. Another estimate is given by Thomas Phillips.

"I have before me the returns for six weeks only, viz., from September 1st to October 10th. During this period there were added to the Calvinistic Methodist churches in the parish, 368; to the Independents, 180; to the Wesleyans, 67; to the Baptists, 40; and to the Episcopal church, 65—making the total number of fresh communicants, or candidates for communion, 720."

From a survey of such figures, it is evident that counties other than Cardiganshire were profoundly influenced by the revival. The effects on the life of the churches, and on the morals of the communities, were also as powerful and as lasting elsewhere as in that county.

A growing concern was expressed at the Calvinistic Methodist Associations held during August and September for the spiritual nurture of the converts. David Morgan and Thomas Edwards gave a report on the state of the churches in Cardiganshire at a session of the South Wales Association which met at Llangeitho on August 3rd. During the first six months of 1859, 6,200 had been added to the churches, 3,595 of them having been already accepted into full membership. In the light of the success of the gospel in many parts of the territory covered by the association, the following message was brought to the association from the elders' session:

"1. The great necessity for prudence on the part of church officers in dealing with the vast numbers which have been added to the churches lately, was discussed, with a view to their instruction and nurture, and to their conviction and correction for their losses and faults. 2. The churches are exhorted to organize the new members to read the 'Confession of Faith', so that they will be thoroughly conversant with the principles and regulations of the denomination."

There were frequent outbursts of "praising" at the preaching services, and the 8 a.m. prayer meeting on August 4th was attended by about 18,000 people. According to J. J. Morgan, this association has been referred to as "the most remarkable ever held in South Wales", and he gives a description of one of the prayer meetings: "As the Severn stream is met and engulfed by the flowing tide, so the prayers offered on the platform by selected brethren were submerged by billows of 'praise' sweeping up from the sea of worshippers surging on the field. Four young men were called into a waggon to lead in prayer, the youngest of whom was a young farmhand of seventeen or so, in uncouth garments inches short at the ankles and wrists; but he might have been a young seraph to judge by the spiritual force which overwhelmed the worshippers as, with uplifted arms and melting voice, he pleaded, 'May the Heavenly Dove descend now on this meadow!' Having prayed himself, the revivalist requested the vast host to spend two minutes in silent prayer. With bowed heads and streaming eyes the thousands responded, and the solemn and intense silence of those moments was as full of eloquence as any episode of this notable association. David Morgan again offered prayer, commending all the servants who were to preach during the day to God, and beseeching especially that the North Wales brethren should be baptised with the revival fire and carry it home.

"A few minutes later, Thomas John, Cilgerran, walked in a field near by lost in reverie. A friend stopped him, and said, 'What a glorious sight that was, when the thousands were engaged in silent prayer at Mr. Morgan's request! Did you ever see anything like it, Mr. John?' He answered solemnly, 'I didn't see one of them: I saw *no one but God*. I am going home,' he said suddenly. 'How terrible is this place! It is too terrible for me. My flesh is too weak to bear this weight of glory . . .'"

According to a contemporary newspaper, the most striking feature was "a pervading and overwhelming solemnity, convincing even the most stoical that eternal realities had come into intimate contact with the men and women present".

The Nonconformist reported similar numbers at the Bangor Association of mid-September, adding that 7,000 had come from Anglesey alone. Moving reports were given of the revival in North Wales, some 700 having been converted in between twelve and fifteen churches. The work had been preceded by an increased longing in the prayer meetings, prayer being a leading characteristic of the revival in most places. Young and old had been touched, and family worship was being restored to its rightful place. The Association felt constrained to urge all its members to promote the work by all possible means, and to consolidate the converts in their most holy faith.

Doubtless, a wide and fruitful stream of blessing flowed from that Association, favourably influencing the rapidity with which the revival spread in North Wales.[5] Thus, the following week the prayer meeting at Bwlan, Caernarvonshire, felt overpowering influences, which broke forth into general outbursts of jubilation and rapture at the young people's prayer meeting on Sunday night, September 25th, and spread from there to the neighbouring villages.

The autumn of 1859

From the Llangeitho Association David Morgan, accompanied by Daniel Evans of Ffos-y-ffin, went to Glamorgan and Monmouth, where they preached extensively and with some considerable success. The arrangements for this itinerary were probably confirmed—if not made—at that Association, for David Morgan had been prevailed upon by delegates from Ebbw Vale, for example, to visit their district of Monmouthshire.

"A deputation waited upon him at the Llangeitho Association in 1859 to invite him to visit Ebbw Vale and district. They were headed by David Hughes, who had arranged his previous tour in the days of his comparative obscurity. The revivalist expressed a fear that he could not arrange a tour in Monmouthshire. 'Look you, David, my boy,' expostulated

[5] See Note, p. 122.

the quaint old deacon, 'we at Ebbw Vale were dealing with you when you were carrying a basket on your arm and trading on a small scale, and now that you have opened an emporium, don't you think that you can turn the cold shoulder to your old customers.' This arrow found a joint in the revivalist's armour, and he yielded at once."

During October and November, David Morgan laboured as revivalist in Caernarvonshire and Anglesey, returning south to Pembrokeshire by early December. The spring of 1860 was spent in Montgomeryshire and Flintshire. Various ministers, full of revival zeal and fire, laboured in Denbighshire, and were instrumental in bringing great blessing to that county. Robert Williams and David Davies together preached in numerous places in the county in October 1859, and again in January 1860.

The first signs of movement in Radnorshire appeared early in November, when the Baptist church at Rhayader commenced nightly prayer meetings. These were blessed, and at the end of the month other Nonconformist bodies had united with them. The Baptist minister, T. L. Davies, could later write of that time:

"Many now became deeply concerned about their souls, and eagerly sought the Lord for mercy, through the blood of Jesus, shed for the remission of sins. It became evident to all that our prayers were answered—that the Spirit was poured out from on high; for almost every night were seen the tears of the penitent, were heard the sobs and sighs of the mourner and broken-hearted, and the cries of those who saw their lost condition."

By the beginning of 1860, this movement had spread, and numerous conversions were recorded from the neighbouring localities, the strongest movement being felt at Presteigne.

It was in November 1859, that Denbighshire received the

heaviest showers of revival blessing, although some places such as Llandudno and Rhyl had been praying and longing for revival since the beginning of the year. The Welsh communities in the Midlands also felt the impetus of the revival and derived much good from it, as at Liverpool, where the spiritual life of the churches received tremendous stimulus from the revival.

Early 1860

At the suggestion of missionaries from India, the second week of January 1860 was set apart by the North Wales Association to pray especially "for a general outpouring of the Holy Spirit, and in thanksgiving for the amazing and blessed awakenings" that were being experienced in so many places in those days. The *Traethodydd* reported that "the great week of prayer" was "truly remarkable, and one that will be forever embossed on Zion's record-book . . . some thousands joined the followers of the Lamb during that week alone, or as a result of their experiences at that time". Many places felt the revival for the first time in that week of prayer, and at other places there were renewed outbreaks of tremendous power.

Although the phenomena of the revival were witnessed in some localities until the end of 1860, they were, in the main, receding and becoming rarer during the autumn months. By 1862, the churches had become resigned to, and absorbed in, the important work of providing for the spiritual needs of the converts. Thus, the influence and success of the revival had grown steadily from its early beginnings in the summer of 1858, until February 1859, after which its growth had become rapid. The summer of 1859 was a period of great successes and notable achievements, reaching their peak, possibly, during the second week of 1860, the week of prayer,

Subsequently the influence of the revival declined, and the remarkable, even extraordinary, manifestations of the Spirit's presence and power became less frequent. The effects of the revival, at the time delightful and heavenly, were, however, to prove themselves to be much more than transient.

5. THE FRUIT OF REVIVAL

BEFORE assessing the results of the 1859 Revival, it is necessary to define broadly the nature of the movement, and to show wherein lay the impact of the Spirit's work felt at that time. The achievements must be measured against the religious situation prevalent before the mighty work commenced.

In this connection, mention has already been made of the orthodoxy of the churches in that period. Many church members, it was noted, had experienced or witnessed previous revivals, and there were some in the churches, ministers and leaders amongst them, who desired revival in 1858. The readiness with which the various churches set themselves to pray for an outpouring of the Spirit when news of the American work reached them was in itself an indication of such a situation obtaining in their midst.

By and large, however, the watchmen on the walls of Zion had fallen asleep, and they were few in number who saw her peril and desperate need. The revival therefore came to the Church as a clarion call, to awaken her out of such a dangerous slumber, and to stir up her members from their lethargic and lukewarm condition. As a direct consequence of this, prayer became more fervent, preaching more powerful, zeal for the conversion of the ungodly more passionate, and godliness more prominent, in her midst. The work of the Spirit in the 1859 revival was therefore primarily the awakening of a sleeping Church, where there had been, and where there was spiritual life, but where the vigorous, healthy evidences of life had seriously subsided and become alarmingly dormant.

The 1859 revival in the experience of the Church could

therefore be compared to the bustle and activity of spring
after a bleak and dark winter. When Zion awoke out of her
slumber under the sunshine of the good pleasure of God and
the refreshing showers of the Holy Spirit, she soon became
a vital, sturdy shoot. Her growth could not be checked, and
as the living sap continued to flow, she transformed the world
with the sweet fragrance of her flowers, and bore much
precious fruit. This new life in the Church soon acted as an
irresistible force in the world, and numbers were added to the
Church who before had been amongst the most profane and
careless. A notable instance of this is given by J. J. Morgan:

"In an evening service, a coarse and callous farmer was
strangely affected. In the morning he was alarmed by the
consciousness of a mysterious and revolutionary change in
himself. *He was unable to swear.* He said to himself like
Samson, 'I will go out as at other times before, and shake
myself'. But his evil strength had departed, and he was weak
and was as another man. He sought his servants at their
work, imagining that he would there find sufficient reasons
for the exercise of his cherished habit, but for the life of him
he couldn't rap out a single oath. Then he realised that his
ailment required a drastic remedy, and thought, as a last
resort, that if he could see some neighbour's sheep trespassing
on his pasture the lost faculty would be recovered. So he
climbed a hill that was near, but nothing availed. He began
to tremble in every limb. 'What is this?' cried he. 'I can't
swear; what if I tried to *pray*?' He fell on his knees among
the furze-bushes, and continued a man of prayer as long as
he lived."

Yet another example is provided by the testimony of one
of the managers of the lead-mines at the end of March 1860:

"I have been here eleven years. Almost all the miners
used to be drunkards and Sabbath-breakers. They would

come to their work on Monday with bruised faces and black eyes. The change is beyond anything I ever knew. I saw great revivals in Cornwall, but none to compare with the present awakening in these parts. They work here in companies of four, six, eight, twelve, and twenty. There is no company without its prayer meeting underground before commencing work. They sing beautifully. On Saturday they gather together underground to render thanks for the mercies of the week. There is scarcely a house without its family altar."

Multitudes of converts

About 110,000 were converted and added to the churches as a result of the 1859 revival in Wales. The Calvinistic Methodist and Congregational churches each received about 36,000 new members; the Baptists about 14,000; the Wesleyans about 5,000, and the Established church about 20,000.

A typical statement of the nature of the work accomplished during the revival is given by Thomas Jones, in October 1859:

"1. The additions to the churches amount to many thousands, far greater than has ever been known in Wales within the same period of time. 2. I have gathered from inquiry that not one person in every fifty of those who have assumed a profession of religion within the last four or six months, has relapsed into the world. 3. The people generally have been solemnised and brought to think of religious things. I asked an individual near Machynlleth whether the *morals* of the people had improved; he replied, 'Oh, dear, yes, entirely', and then turned to his wife for confirmation of his statement. 'Yes,' she said, 'they are; every day is a Sunday now.' 4. A missionary spirit has taken possession of the churches. There is no limit to their desire to save the whole world. 5. The ministers and preachers are anointed with fresh zeal, and are animated with a new spirit. The churches and their office-bearers are filled with the ardour of their 'first love'. 6. There is a great increase of brotherly love amongst professing Christians, and more cordial co-operation amongst the various denominations in their efforts to do good, and to oppose the common enemy. These are undoubted facts; and I am sure they have not been produced by Satan; nor could they be effected by men without aid from above."

Lasting benefits

The effects thus noted were not transient, but left a lasting, beneficial impression on the state of the Church. The faithfulness and perseverance of the converts, which may be clearly demonstrated, may be regarded as an index of the depth of the work. The Rev. John Jones, also writing in October 1859, could report of those who were joining the churches in Cardiganshire, that they did so only after much deliberation.[6] In 1860 Thomas Phillips made the following observations regarding the methods adopted in the revival:

"On every occasion care is taken to instruct the people in the true and unchangeable principles of religion. They are cautioned against resting in a mere outward profession. They are told that excitement is not conversion, that an awakening of the conscience to a sense of guilt and danger does not always result in a change of heart. It is strongly and constantly urged that whatever hope or confidence they may have in their own minds as to their having 'passed from death unto life', it is a mistake, a delusion, unless it is accompanied by hatred to sin, and a renunciation of it in every shape or form; love to holiness, and the practical discharge of every moral duty. They are told that the Bible is to be the standard of

[6] See Note, p. 123.

religious feeling, as it is of religious faith. In short, they are admonished to seek a thorough change of heart, and to furnish evidence thereof in holiness of life."

Consequently, one estimate, cited in 1897, is that nineteen out of every twenty of the converts maintained their profession and were fruitful in godly duties.

In the Calvinistic Methodist Associations, as the revival progressed, more and more concern was expressed over the care of the converts. As early as the Holyhead Association of March 1859 the ministers and elders of the churches had been exhorted to see to the building up of those newly received into fellowship. A similar resolution at the Llangeitho Association of August 1859 was reiterated at the Llaneirwg Association of September. The Mold Association of March 1860 emphasised the importance of an efficient pastoral ministry in the churches and the Dolgelley Association the following June made strong recommendation that the converts should be catechised on the basis of Thomas Charles's *Hyfforddwr*.[7]

One of the sessions of the Caernarvon Association of September 1860 was given to a discussion of the wisdom and solemnity which should accompany the receiving of new members into the church, the discipline of the church, the choice of elders, and the selection of candidates for the ministry. At the same Association, a suggestion was made that the first week of 1861 should be set apart as a week of prayer. This was ratified at the Holyhead Association of December, and a similar measure was adopted at the South Wales October Association, held at Llanwrtyd.

The concern had not diminished in June 1861, although the Beaufort Association held at the beginning of that month confessed that the greatest need was for the presence of "another Comforter" in the services of the churches. The

North Wales Association held at Pwllheli during September, however, looked upon the revival as already past, but still having lasting and beneficial effects. Amongst these effects are particularly mentioned the increase in family worship, attendance at the means of grace, the cause of temperance and brotherly love.

Family worship

Family worship certainly received tremendous impetus from the revival. Where before this Scriptural practice had been burdensome and unprofitable, with the experiences of the revival it came to be a time of spiritual delight and refreshment. In very many homes where the practice was new, it became a source of spiritual nourishment to the young converts, consolidating and enforcing the blessings received at the means of grace. "The general establishment of family worship is another blessed result of the present awakening," wrote Thomas Phillips in 1860. He continued:

"This is expected from all the converts, and they set about it forthwith. They are told that they must not rest satisfied with prayer and praise in the public sanctuary, but that God must be worshipped in their own houses by their assembled families; and, as in the case of Abraham, Jehovah must have an altar in their dwelling. Inability and timidity are not admitted as excuses. They must *try*."

Indeed, the widespread setting up of family worship was put forward in the early stages of the revival as evidence of the authenticity of the work. Thus a correspondent of the *Drysorfa*, "one of the children of the revival", from Ysbyty Ystwyth, commends the work on this basis as early as January 1859. A similar claim was made in April of the same year by another correspondent reporting on the revival, and the Reverend John Jones related that the new converts in Cardiganshire were not slow to train their families in religious exercises.

The cause of temperance also received a stimulus from the revival, and the influence upon the "drink market" was such that, at Bala for example, the revival was regarded almost as a "temperance revival". Until the time of the revival, the efforts of the temperance societies had been ineffective, but as a result of that supernatural visitation, great numbers were converted. Their subsequent allegiance to the temperance movements was a direct effect of the revival, and not the cause of it. Here is Thomas Phillips' summary of the situation:

"Notwithstanding the great efforts made in times past to stem the torrent by means of 'temperance' and 'total abstinence' societies, drunkenness continued to an alarming extent . . . even professedly religious people were too often found amongst the frequenters of public-houses . . . It was at this juncture that the revival broke forth;—at the time when godly people feared that the tide of intemperance, instead of ebbing, was flowing in more rapidly, another agency was raised up to arrest its progress. Although total abstinence is not made a condition of membership in any church, it is strongly recommended to the new candidates, whether young or old, both as a safeguard to themselves and as an example to others."

Unity amongst churches

Another effect of the revival was the unity manifested amongst the several denominations, particularly the Nonconformist bodies. This unity arose from two main sources; the one, an agreement as to the basic truths of the gospel, and the other, a common, fervent desire for a visitation of the Holy Spirit to glorify Christ as Saviour and Lord.

Inasmuch as each denomination based its faith and

practice at that time upon God's revealed truth, as found in
Holy Scripture, their unity did not involve the violation of
any of their distinctive principles, nor the surrender of
any essential belief, as these were already common to all.
Consequently, their prayer meetings and joint services were
eminently useful in furthering the work of the revival, being
soundly based on essential, divinely-revealed truth.   At
Presteigne, for example, all the Nonconformists of the town
met to pray for the divine visitation "without any semblance
of sectarianism".

"All deeply felt the necessity of prayer—of united prayer
and effort for the conversion of precious souls; and hence the
house of prayer became a delightful resort . . . This had a
marked influence on the world; for, in addition to the earnest
spirit of prayer which prevailed, they saw that an earnest spirit
of *united* prayer and *united* effort for their salvation prevailed.
They saw that it was no longer the movement of a party or
of a sect; but that all the true from all the sects had but one
common object in view, namely, the conversion of their souls
—the glory of Christ."

Such were some of the more general fruits of the 1859
Revival.   There were many more, some of them of a more
particular nature, and others so significant as to become
leading characteristics of the movement.

All age groups affected

People of all ages experienced the blessings of the revival,
and the predominance of any age group was local rather than
national. Morgan's momentary inspiration in dealing with one
of the older converts is illustrated by the following incident:
"A decrepit old sinner named Harry left before the church
meeting and climbed a part of his hilly way homewards. He
was found later hanging about the chapel door, and explained

falteringly that it was too dark to go home without company. He entered and walked straight 'to his own place'—the bench of the penitents. 'Well! well!' said David Morgan to him, 'your hair is very white.' 'Yes, it is,' acknowledged Harry. 'Did you once have black hair, tell me?' 'Yes, black as jet.' 'And who got the black hair from you?' 'The old devil, every hair,' answered Harry. 'Oh! the pity of it!' lamented the revivalist. 'The black curls of youth a gift to the devil, and only a few withered wisps of white hair for Jesus Christ! But God will accept the white hair from this to the end.' 'Thank Him!' sobbed Harry."

There were many old people in the congregation at Blaencefn. One of these, William Thomas, "a man of blameless walk, a great reader, a fine theologian, the best teacher in the Sabbath-school, and a man who conducted family worship regularly, was the last of the veterans to bend. One evening he rose in his pew to leave, halted for a space by the big seat, then hardened his face and proceeded as far as the door, turned back, hesitating, but finally passed out into the court in front. He pulled up there again for a few minutes, then dragged his unwilling feet as far as the gate leading to the roadway. Once again he stopped short, listening to the music within. Stepping forward, his white locks floating on the breeze, he was heard soliloquizing despairingly, 'Oh! there is no one on the road but the devil and myself!' A few moments later he added, 'This is the most terrible war I was ever in!' Before day-break David Evans, shoemaker and deacon, heard a loud knock at his door, and a peremptory cry—'David Evans, how can you sleep in such a storm as this?' The distracted veteran was admitted, and after the reading of Scripture and prayer, the tempest-tossed soul found Him who is a hiding-place from the wind."

At Fishguard the first manifestations of the revival were felt through the prayers of young children. Children played a leading part in bringing the revival to Llanllechid, St. Dogmaels and Dinorwig, and at Aberystwyth, Bangor, Bryneglwys and Saron, near Denbigh, some of the most powerful influences were felt at children's prayer meetings. A child convert at Rhosesmor was heard to pray, "My father is ungodly; I am afraid to go home because of his swearing. O! come and save him, Lord! Thou hast knocked at his door many times; compel him to open, and if he refuses, take the door off its hinges, Lord!"

The Congregationalist minister, W. Evans of Aberaeron, could report on May 16th, 1859, that one "of the most striking characteristics" of the movement was its effect on "young people, and even on children". He continues:

"The youth of our congregations are nearly all the subjects of deep religious impressions. Many of them seem as if filled with the Spirit of prayer. Very young people, yea, children from ten to fourteen years of age, gather together to hold prayer meetings, and pray very fervently . . . When it happens . . . that children only, or servants profess spiritual piety in a family, they instantly crave permission to have family prayer, and thus divine worship is established in nearly every family in the country."

The remarkable manifestations of divine power witnessed at Llanharan were prefaced by an influx into the church of children between eight and ten years of age, who sought admission "under powerful impressions". John Davies, minister of the Congregational church at Aberaman, referred to this work as follows: "I heard Mr. Griffiths, the minister, say that the reviving influence appeared too weak to move the old swearers and inveterate sinners, and that he compared the children to steam-tugs sent out to draw large vessels into port. After this, such a power was experienced as to move the hardest and the worst of sinners". At another place, "One morning at eight, little children held a prayer meeting on behalf of an aged sinner of eighty-four who was locally known as 'Old Aberleri'. That same day in the afternoon service the old rebel yielded, conquered by love divine and human. 'Bring forth the best robe,' cried the revivalist joyfully; 'his Father has seen him'. He was absolutely illiterate, but as a new-born babe he desired the sincere milk of the Word. He obtained it in halfpenny-worths by giving coppers to any children who would read a chapter to him."

Thomas Edwards visited Dolgelley in April 1859, and reported on the progress of the revival in Cardiganshire. David Morgan and Evan Phillips followed him in June, but their ministries were comparatively unsuccessful. It was not until the night of November 4th, 1859, that the full impact of the revival was felt at Dolgelley, and it came upon a children's prayer meeting in the vestry of the Calvinistic Methodist chapel. The minister was sent for, and later described the scene which he witnessed on arriving at the vestry, and the amazing experiences of the Sunday which followed:

"I saw there the most terrible spectacle of my experience; some on their knees, and some on their faces completely overpowered. The succeeding week was a strange one, and the following Sabbath was unparalleled to me and terrible to the Dolgelley congregation. There were loud outcries from souls in agony, and thirty-five sought a place in God's house."

In many places the young people held a prayer meeting of their own, and these sometimes proved instrumental in bringing the powerful influences of the revival to that particular locality. Such was the case at Hermon, Mynydd Llandygái and Capel Hirael, Blaen-cefn, Denbigh and Rhyl. The majority of the converts of the revival at Neuadd-lwyd and Rhosllannerchrugog were young people; and at Llanwrtyd and

Dinas Mawddwy they were the first-fruits of the gracious visitation of God's Spirit to those localities.

Richard Owen (the "revivalist") was twenty years old when he heard David Morgan preaching at Llangristiolus in 1859, and his experiences at that time strengthened his resolution to preach. He was greatly used in 1883 in the revival which broke out at that time in Caernarvonshire, and which spread to many Welsh counties. Thomas Charles Edwards, who was to become first Principal of the University College of Wales at Aberystwyth, and a renowned preacher and expositor, was twenty-two years of age, and a theological student at Bala, in 1859. He had commenced preaching in 1856, but David Morgan's visit to Bala in 1859 proved to be pivotal to his spiritual and ministerial career. This was his testimony at David Morgan's funeral in 1883:

"I was in College at the time studying great matters, but never having realised them in my experience as living truth. I knew Butler's arguments for a future state, and Paley's *Evidences of Christianity*. I felt their force as arguments. But here came two plain men from Cardiganshire to Bala, and preached Jesus Christ simply and unaffectedly, without much culture or eloquence: but they had more. Eternity pervaded the service, heaven was in the place . . . no one needed Butler's arguments or Paley's Evidences. The change that I experienced was ample evidence to me of the divinity of Christianity. Before, I was a mass of damnation, and in the service I became a new creature."

From the consideration of these instances, it is evident that the effects of the revival were both profound and lasting. Indeed, the whole character and course of Nonconformity for the subsequent years of the century were to a great extent determined by that remarkable work.

Similar features in revivals elsewhere

The remarkable times of refreshing experienced in other countries, such as America, Ireland, Scotland and England, displayed similar characteristics, but in each case there were distinctive features. A fervency in, and frequency of, prayer meetings, was generally apparent in most of the contemporary movements, while physical manifestations were especially prominent in, and more particularly confined to, Ireland. In Wales the revival was initiated and promoted by means of prayer, together with the labours of Humphrey Jones, David Morgan and other itinerant ministers. This itinerant ministry of the Nonconformist bodies lent itself readily to a propagation of the revival fire.

While the Welsh work displayed many characteristics common to other contemporary revivals, it was to a large extent independent of them. It is true that the Welsh revival was instigated by news of the American work. It was also related to it through Humphrey Jones, who had been fired with revival zeal as a direct result of the American work, but the work in Wales followed its own distinctive course, and developed along certain clearly-defined and typical lines.

The only instance where the Irish Revival was immediately and intimately responsible for initiating a similar work in Wales was at Thorne, Pembrokeshire. Early in 1860, a young girl returned to Thorne from a visit to Ulster, full of the spirit of the revival which was sweeping through the churches there, and, together with some friends, she attended a prayer meeting in the Wesleyan chapel. "In that meeting the young girl poured out her heart in prayer, the like of which was never before heard in that locality." As a result of that meeting, at least one person was converted, and a number of prayer meetings were started in the chapels and in the homes. The effects of the revival soon spread and many were converted. J. Edwin Orr summarises the position thus:

"It can be demonstrated that the Welsh Revival of 1859 was almost wholly unrelated, historically and geographically, to the Irish and Scottish Revivals of the same period. It owed nothing to them. However, the Welsh Revival of 1859 displayed many features of spiritual kinship with the contemporary movements in Ireland and Scotland, and all three derived inspiration from the American movement in 1858."

As the revival progressed in Wales, it came to have its own prominent men, and to display its own characteristics.

The pre-eminence of prayer

Prayer was undoubtedly one of the leading characteristics of the revival in Wales, as it was in many other countries. The powerful influences of the revival were first felt, and continued to be felt, generally, in the prayer meetings. A strong—sometimes overwhelming—influence would pervade the meeting while someone prayed, or during the singing of a hymn in the prayer meeting. This movement would be felt by all present, manifesting itself in different ways; bringing some to an overpowering sense of guilt and conviction of sin, and creating in others an irresistible desire to rejoice in and praise the God of their salvation. Such remarkable impressions were not transitory, but were the means of bringing vast numbers to a saving faith in Christ, and bringing into the experience of countless Christians a new, fervent desire for the salvation of the ungodly.

Hence, David Charles could list as the three main characteristics of the revival the following: "Firstly, an extraordinary spirit of prayer among the masses; secondly, a remarkable spirit of union among all denominations of Christians; and thirdly, a powerful missionary effort for the conversion of others". A correspondent of the *Drysorfa* for April 1859, reports thus regarding this outstanding feature of the revival:

"The amazing thing is, that those meetings which were attended by the fewest people . . . the prayer meetings,— those are now predominant. In a real way, it is the Spirit of prayer which is poured out upon us in these days". These sentiments were reiterated as the revival progressed, so that in 1860, the same monthly organ of the Calvinistic Methodist church bears repeated notices of the prevalence and success of the prayer meetings. Under a revival report concerning Llangefni, for example, there appears the following statement:

"The great fruit of this revival is prayer. It was preceded by prayer, and it issues in prayer, which remains its chief agent. In previous awakenings, the ministry of the Word was the chief means . . . but the particular means of this present movement is 'the prayer';—everyone is coming to believe in the efficacy of prayer . . ."

The *Annibynwr* for January 1860 carried a similar notice, and Thomas Phillips, after personal inquiry into the principal features of the revival gives as his conclusion the following estimate, which he substantiates by quoting a correspondent:

"Without disparaging the pulpit, or in any way degrading the offices instituted by Christ in His Church, it must strike all, that *prayer*, oral, united prayer, has been greatly honoured of God, as a means of commencing and extending the present movement . . . A correspondent says:—'We expected that the great outpouring of the Spirit would come by means of preaching. It was so in former days—it may be so again— and is so now, to some extent. Thank God, the ministry has not lost its power; but still, it is quite clear that the Holy Spirit's influence, at the present time, is communicated by means of prayer."

Insistence on preaching

At no time during the revival, however, were the prayer meetings allowed to replace or exclude the preaching of the

Word. The experiences of the revival were thus tempered with a sound knowledge of the truth, and many undesirable excesses and errors were thereby avoided. Indeed, it was the insistence of David Morgan, and the other leading ministers engaged in the work, on preaching, that delivered the movement from those spurious manifestations which might have given weight to the objections levelled against the work by some. Here are the most frequently occurring complaints.

"It is a man-made revival; the chief instruments in it are not persons of any weight or character; women and children are the subjects of it; it is mere excitement and enthusiasm, and although many persons of disreputable conduct seem to be for the present changed, yet, when the excitement ceases, they will return to their former habits, and their end will be worse than their beginning . . . it will be said, the *noise*—the *confusion*—the loud and long prayers—and singing, with various excesses of feeling, and extravagance of language,— these are most offensive . . . The 'converts' . . . will ere long be 'perverts'. They will go back, betray religion and bring disgrace on the whole movement."

The insistence upon the preaching of the Word, together with a rigid examination of the spiritual experience of the converts before acceptance into full membership of the Church, and an efficient programme of catechising the converts, did much to prove such objections false and unfounded. Thus, the churches' emphasis on the importance of caring for the spiritual welfare of new members was not without its reasons or effects, for as a result, the growth of the movement and its subsequent course proved to be both healthy and vigorous.

Methods employed

An objection was also registered against the way in which David Morgan normally proceeded at the close of a meeting.

It was considered to be detrimental to the work because it was maintained that by that method the numbers of spurious conversions would be considerably higher than would otherwise be the case. Thomas Edwards described David Morgan's method thus:

"First he would preach for a short while from the pulpit, and then, generally, close with a prayer. After singing a hymn he would come down from the pulpit to the big seat— or perhaps into the midst of the congregation—to speak to the ungodly in a most searching and purposeful manner. Each time he gives men an opportunity to join the church, should any so desire."

John Jones later defended this method as being effective to impress upon those present that the preacher was addressing his remarks to them personally. He continued:

"It may be after all, that there isn't here as much innovation as might appear at first sight, for on the whole, there was nothing new in these addresses, which had not been heard before . . . since they had been delivered time and time again by the fathers and by contemporary brethren. The greatest innovation was in the spirit of the preacher . . . The difference between the present method and that of the past was not in the act of the preacher in descending from the pulpit to the 'big seat', but in the power of the spirit with which he was anointed; in a word, the Spirit of the Lord was being poured out."

It is interesting to note that, in order to avoid the disastrous effects of superficial conversions and artificial, unreal professions, David Morgan changed the nature of some of the meetings during the early period at Pont-rhyd-y-groes. "He established meetings of a more edifying nature on particular evenings to discuss the basic principles of religion, so as to strengthen and cultivate the converts." Someone would be appointed to open discussion by preparing and delivering a short address on the subject, and the resulting exchange of opinions and expositions would prove profitable and stimulating. In spite of these attempts to avert criticisms and objections directed against David Morgan and the converts, when the revivalist visited Cardiff in September 1859, many charged him with "Finneyism" because of his method of addressing the unconverted in the personal and intimate manner noted. It was said that the churches would be filled with "carnal men", who had experienced only a temporary and external change in their conduct, and that in their hearts they were still unregenerate. According to one report, hundreds were added to the churches as a result of David Morgan's visit. His work was later consolidated and extended by the preaching tour of Evan Evans and John Owens through Glamorganshire in January 1860.

Under the inspired preaching of the Word and the powerful, humbling influences of the Spirit in the prayer meetings, the congregations became earnest and disturbed about spiritual matters. Such solemnity was felt in the church and at home, in conversation and in the society. Men who had been stubborn, indifferent and sceptical were moved to the very foundation of their being. They were as though terrorised by thoughts of God and of the world to come, by thoughts of death and judgment. Their remorse because of mis-spent time and past opposition to a loving Saviour knew no bounds. Upon finding deliverance in the merits of a crucified Saviour, their lives were changed, and such regenerated lives soon gave evidence of being under a new master.

Changed style of preaching

These amazing effects were produced under the preaching of the Word, the whole tenor of which was radically changed during the revival. As early as February 1859, Thomas

Edwards could assess this change in the style of the preaching thus:

"This revival has made a great change in the style of preaching, and in the spirit of the preacher. It would appear that the object is, more than ever, to preach the substantial truths of the gospel, so earnestly, closely and personally, that the hearers may feel that the preacher's aim is to save their souls, and that God, by *His* means, desires to bring them to Himself. The people are compelled to believe this. The preacher comes near them . . . It is not a fight at arm's length, but the preacher advances immediately to the people, lays hold of them, and they feel that the sermon has entered into them, and that the preacher has taken possession of the throne of their hearts in the name of Jesus. The awakened minister is as much engaged in seeking to save souls out of the pulpit as in it. He exhorts, he presses the truth upon them, and prays with them."

From this estimate it is evident that, prior to the revival, the preaching of the Word had degenerated into a theoretical, oratorical presentation of the truth, lacking urgency and sincerity. It was designed to please the congregation, and to win applause to the preacher, but not to move men to repentance nor to stimulate faith in a risen Saviour. According to one report which appeared in the *Annibynwr* for April 1859, the revival wrought a manifest change in the tone and style of the preaching in this way, "Instead of prosaical preaching, delivered in a formal and lifeless manner, the preacher sets himself to speak freely and directly with the people about their state". This statement corresponds to that given by Evan Davies:

"When we look back some years previous to this gracious visitation, the churches were very deficient in spirituality. There was no relish for the plain heart-searching truths of the gospel. They wanted things new, strange, uttered in a refined style, when they would admire the ability of the man, but not the great things of God. And I fancied very often that there was too much tendency in the ministry to indulge this craving in the people."

The revival thus restored to preaching a note of urgency, and ministers were enabled to bring into focus the essential truths of Christianity. Their message, under the especial anointing of the Holy Spirit, was delivered with plainness, earnestness and tremendous power. As a result of the proclamation of plain gospel truths, delivered without any embellishment of man, and with that simplicity which is in Christ, the settling of eternal issues became a matter of gravity and priority.

Bishop MacIlvaine, described as "one of the most eminent Prelatists of the American Episcopal Church", maintained that two lessons could be learned from the 1859 revival in America.

"1. That the gospel is now, in its profoundest simplicity, what it was in the days of the apostles, namely, the wisdom and power of God unto salvation. If it is in any sense old, having led God's people through so many wilderness wanderings and dangers . . . its eye has not yet darkened, nor has its power weakened. It does not require the wisdom of man to make it more timely to the modern situation, or to any class of men. The hearts and consciences of men in the nineteenth century, and amongst the most enlightened of the worldly-wise, are in as much need of the gospel, yea, and are just as easily humbled by it, as its hearers in the first years of its growth. What is needed in the preaching of the gospel, is to expound it simply and fully, and to apply it with purpose to the minds and hearts of the people, with all the love, faith and zeal that the preacher can muster in his ministry. 2. The power of prayer, and the importance of gathering together to pray . . . Prayer meetings have been the wings of this movement. And the Word has been fuel to it. God has honoured the one and the other."

As in America, so also in Wales, that preaching was signally honoured and mightily used which gave central place to the saving truths of the gospel, applied in a plain but moving manner. Thomas Phillips made these observations on the work in Wales in 1860:

"When the public ministry has been the means of conversion in the present movement, it has been of that character which the Holy Spirit ever delights to honour with success— the simple exhibition of gospel truths, poured forth from a heart full of love to Christ. The revival has come just in time to arrest a growing tendency in some quarters to substitute the wisdom of man for the grace of God, the philosophy of the schools for the cross of Christ, well-prepared essays and elaborate compositions for the good, old-fashioned, preaching of Christ and His cross."

Supremely, therefore, the revival restored the ministry to its New Testament prestige and vigour, and as a direct result of this, the preaching of the Word became at once both authoritative and fruitful. By this means God's people were awakened to a keen sense of their privileges and responsibilities, while the ungodly were presented with God's gracious offer of justification by faith and a full, eternal salvation in the meritorious death of the Son of God. The scenes and experiences which resulted from such an inspired proclamation of gospel truths were often compared to those of New Testament times, and from this demonstration of the function and efficacy of the ministerial office the following important principles were deduced.

"The present revival has broken down the tyranny of form, fashion and shame. The gospel, properly preached, lived and applied, is irresistible. The Church . . . ought never have descended to apologise, to mince truth, or to be afraid to live and to follow it out . . . The secret of success is belief . . . in the personal verification of gospel truths . . . that God meant with an infinite intensity and divine earnestness every syllable that He ever spoke, and a belief that His sayings are to be realised to us and through us . . . The consciousness of inward failings and weaknesses must be outweighed by the conscious assurance of God's choice of such instrumentality to renew the world. The apostles had their failings—the Reformers had their weaknesses, but, instead of waiting till they arrived at the consciousness of perfection, they relied upon God, and went forth in His strength."

These were elements which came to the fore in the preaching of the Word during the 1859 revival. They may be summed up in the dictum of one of Thomas Phillips' correspondents, "If we had more life and earnestness in the pulpit, there would be far more life and holiness in the congregations."

A time of harvest

The revival was a time of harvest in the churches, when the fruit of many years' labour was being gathered. For this reason, in any assessment of the cause or success of the work, account must be taken of the faithful preaching of the years preceding that time of "refreshing". The days of the mighty men of the pulpit had long since passed, but during the decade or two before 1859, the Church had been blessed with the ministry of some faithful men. These had preached the truth without compromise or fear, but at the time had witnessed little success to their labours. This fact was noted at the Bangor Association of March 1859, when the time of revival was referred to as "a time of harvest" in the Church, and that "the effects of thirty years labour had been brought to fruition in that period". *Baner Cymru* echoed those words in an article which was reprinted in the *Drysorfa*: "It is an evident fact that the backbone of the present awakening in Wales is the ministry of the thirty years which have passed. We see now that the preaching of Williams of Wern, Ebenezer Morris, John Elias and others, is still alive."

These sentiments were again expressed at the Bangor Association of September:

"There is no room to suppose that what some maintain, that the praying has taken the place of the preaching and that nothing is wrought by the ministry of the gospel, is true; rather, the fruits of the preaching of twenty years or more are now being received by the Church in answer to prayer. Many who come afresh to the churches are heard to say that sermons which they heard some fifteen or more years since, had clung to their minds, and continued to wound them more and more, until they now had to give themselves to the Lord and to His people."

Robert Ellis was of the same opinion:

"Rather than that anything in the features of this revival tends to debase the ministry of the Word, there are countless evidences in it to the contrary, namely, that in the last resort, it was only a great ingathering of the fruit of the previous years' preaching. While listening to the numbers of converts relating their experience, they confess, almost without exception, that some word or observation in a sermon which they had heard some considerable time ago, had persisted in their consciences, in spite of all the pomp of their irreligious life."

Conclusions

Several factors could be noted as instrumental in the good providence of God, and under His sovereign disposition, in bringing about the 1859 revival in Wales, and in contributing to its tremendous success. The preaching of the Word faithfully in the period leading up to 1859; the prayers of God's people immediately preceding the awakening; the influence of the American work, both in stimulating prayer and through the labours of Humphrey Jones; the work of David Morgan as revivalist; the itinerant ministries of many others; and the readiness of the churches, through their ecclesiastical courts, to provide for the welfare of the converts; all these elements combined to give the Welsh revival of 1859 its distinctive character and its permanent value.

From this summary of the achievements of the work, some leading, basic principles regarding God's dealings with His Church are at once evident. From a consideration of the facts relating to the manner of God's dealings with men at that time the efficacy of fervent, resolute and importunate prayer can hardly be denied. It is equally clear that the proclamation of the truth can never be apologetic; it will always be dogmatic, authoritative and successful. Furthermore, he will never be fruitful in his ministry who preaches any other gospel than that of the New Testament apostles. Truth never changes, and the compromise of truth is a total betrayal of it to error, and this half-truth, being also half-error, is in itself contradictory to the whole truth, and therefore inevitably hostile to it.

There are but few elements in the religious situation today which are comparable to those of 1859. Wales can hardly be referred to as the "land of revivals" during this century, for since the divine visitation of 1904-5, there have been no further widespread movements of the Holy Spirit. Again, unlike the Church of 1858, the Church of today looks back upon a period of dearth in powerful, authoritative preaching. To an alarming extent, divine revelation has been supplanted by human invention, and the latter has proved itself neither conducive nor satisfying to godliness. Supernatural Christianity has been abandoned as untenable and incompatible with the "enlightened" and so-called "scientific" mind. The basic facts and essential principles of Christianity have been surrendered as either untrue or unnecessary, with the result that the historic, dogmatic and saving truths of the Christian faith have been regarded as useless and old-fashioned.

During the 1859 revival there was an unmistakable reversion to the plain preaching of the saving truths of the gospel. What God had honoured in New Testament times through the apostles' preaching of Christ crucified, and of forgiveness of sins in the merit of Christ's finished work, He was pleased to bless in the time of the Reformers, of the Puritans, of the Methodists, and of David Morgan. God has not changed; His gospel has not changed; His promises have not changed. May He lead His servants to seek Him, to preach His revealed truth, and to claim His unchangeable promises.

"O Lord, though our iniquities testify against us, do thou it for thy name's sake: for our backslidings are many: we have sinned against thee. O the hope of Israel, the saviour thereof in time of trouble, why shouldest thou be as a stranger in the land, and as a wayfaring man that turneth aside to tarry for a night? Why shouldest thou be as a man astonied, as a mighty man that cannot save? yet thou, O Lord, art in the midst of us, and we are called by thy name; leave us not" (Jeremiah 14: 7-9).

NOTES

1. In this interesting letter, William Williams says: "The bible, which I used to read, in a great measure, for the edification of others, I now apply entirely to myself, as the only book by which I shall be tried in the great judgment . . . I have come to see that true religion consists of three parts: first, true light respecting the plan of salvation; God's eternal covenant with His Son to pay the debt of believing sinners, all the truths of the new Covenant by which he becomes all in all in creation, in all-embracing providence, and in redemption . . . The books of Dr. Goodwin, Dr. Owen, Dr. Gill, Marshall, Harvey, Usher, and others, have helped to enliven my understanding of these great truths; but now, in this affliction of mine, I have come to see that I am very defective in a subject not less magnificent than the other, that is, being in intimate fellowship with God in all our dealings with the world, and in all the exercises and ordinances of religion . . . The scriptures which convey the promise of the Holy Spirit contain promises of this heavenly fellowship with God; and as the Holy Spirit is promised in some measure to every believer, this communion is the inheritance of every true Christian . . . I have now, in my affliction, seen that I fall very short of this peaceful fellowship, which is like heaven on Earth; and I have had reasons for believing that there are multitudes of professors, eminent in the world's esteem, who make hardly any effort to attain this heavenly element, sad to say. Lastly, I have come to see the third part of true religion—life and conduct, such as would reveal to the ungodly that there is a great difference between us and them".

2. The debt of the Methodist "fathers" to the Puritans of the seventeenth century does not seem to have been hitherto appreciated, and can hardly be over-estimated. Here are a few instances of this: Daniel Rowland translated into Welsh, among other things, *The Holy War*, by John Bunyan; Howel Harris often read the works of the Puritans, such as William Bates on the *Harmony of the Divine Attributes*, and Thomas Coles on *Regeneration, Faith and Repentance*. William Williams was indebted to many of the Puritan divines for enlivening his understanding of the great truths of the New Covenant and published in 1779 *Hanes Troedigaeth* . . .

Thomas Goodwin; Thomas Charles drew extensively from Puritan authors for his *Geiriadur Ysgrythyrol* (Scriptural Dictionary), as a survey of the footnotes to its articles will show. Thus, for example, the article on "Adenedigaeth" (Regeneration) is partly based on Part I of Isaac Ambrose's *Works* which deals with "The Doctrine of Regeneration, or the New Birth". Thomas Jones of Denbigh completed the translation of *The Christian in Complete Armour* by William Gurnal by bringing out the Third Part in 1796, and the Fourth Part in 1809.

3. J. J. Morgan says that the first general expression of jubilation and praising broke out after a Sunday School festival held at Bronnant sometime in mid-March, many members from Blaenpennal being present. "That night a prayer meeting was held at Blaenpennal and although it was a tempestuous night, a multitude of people attended . . . While singing ' 'Rhwn sy'n gyrru'r mellt i hedeg, &c.' ('He who speeds the lightning flashes, &c.') there was a general confusion. The place was momentarily overcome by a heavenly disorder. The rejoicing and shouting in the chapel was chaotic. Those who shouted were only rarely visible. They lay prostrate in the dust, and only an arm occasionally thrown over the back of the seat in front would be seen. For ten months afterwards hardly a meeting would pass without an outburst of general jubilation."

4. The efficacy of prayer had also been impressed upon the Presbyterian Church in Ireland, and in the May Synod of Armagh and Monaghan which met at Portadown, Co. Armagh, the following suggestions were made: "(*a*) 'That ministers should prayerfully bear in their hearts the conviction that souls are perishing around them, that the Lord has, in a special manner, committed into their hands the Bread of Life and that it is incumbent on them, aided by their sessions and the godly members of their congregations, to use the utmost diligence to bring the unconverted to Christ, ever realising the great gospel truth that men are only instruments and that without the Holy Spirit sent down from heaven nothing can be effectually accomplished'; (*b*) 'That sessions should meet frequently and wherever practicable, statedly for prayer, for conference on the state of religion in their respective congregations, for devising means for the promotion of vital godliness within their bounds'. (*c*) 'That while we strongly urge the necessity of increased attention to private, family and public supplication to God for the outpouring of the Holy Spirit, we would also earnestly recommend the establishment

of special congregational meetings for the reading of God's Word and for prayer, to which elders and also members of the church whom God has gifted with the Spirit of prayer and the gift of utterance, shall be invited and encouraged to take part'."

5. Here is an account of the amazing scenes witnessed as a crowd of about 30,000 listened to the powerful preaching of the Reverend John Jones of Blaenannerch at Bangor. "The preacher read his text in a low and trembling voice, and for ten minutes it seemed doubtful whether he would not sink beneath his burden . . . His text was, 'Behold, I lay in Zion for a foundation a stone, a tried stone, &c.' (Isaiah 28: 16). 'A *tried* stone?' he cried; 'this stone has been tried very severely. I see the world and hell assaulting it. The sun grew black, rocks rent, and graves opened when the stone was under the test, but it bore all without a flaw. Build on this stone. I behold riches taking wing, health failing, friends departing, but the Stone does not move—a SURE Foundation' . . . His sweet and sonorous voice now reaches a pitch that wakes the echo in a neighbouring cliff, and every rapturous shout in praise of the Stone of Israel is redoubled with quaint effect by the Bangor Rock. 'Salvation is of God.' 'Behold I lay.' God Himself handled the square and the compass in shaping and laying this Stone. Every inch of it bears the stamp of heaven. Wouldn't you like to try it, you lads of the quarries? You must come to Zion to find it. The Son of God will not be found in the theatre; the Stone is not in the taverns, my boys; life is not found in the palaces of iniquity. If you want to build on the Stone, make the best of your way to Zion. This Stone is God's appointment . . . 'Whom God hath set forth to be a propitiation'; 'I have found a ransom'. 'What a glorious word for an Association, *Ransom*', cries the preacher . . . 'This word fills a field, *Ransom* . . . This word fills the world, RANSOM . . . It fills eternity—RANSOM . . .' The preacher's magnificent voice . . . was steeped in heavenly unction, and it made the multitudinous souls under its spell like the chariots of Amminadib (Song of Solomon, 6: 12). For some time the minister had been preaching to an accompaniment of many voices in the audience, like ominous drops that herald a cloudburst. Then came his mighty, melodious shouts of '*Ransom*, RANSOM, RANSOM,' and—*after that the flood*. Some who were present told us that the rapture and thunder often arose on the fringe of the vast host, travelled like an irresistible wave towards the preacher, its course marked by lifted hands, hats, and handkerchiefs waved in the air, swoons and outcries; and broke at last in spray, as it were, over the platform, where the ministers

sat . . . It [that service] was the means of bringing scores, if not hundreds, to build for eternity on the Rock of Ages."

6. An example of a "decision card" in use during the 1859 revival in Ireland is in the form of a "Covenant", based upon Scriptural references. Here it is:

"MY COVENANT

I take God the Father to be my God (1 Thessalonians 1: 9)
I take Christ the Son to be my Saviour (Acts 5: 31)
I take the Holy Spirit to be my Sanctifier (1 Peter 1: 2)
I take the Word of God to be my Rule (2 Timothy 3: 16)
I take the people of God to be my people (Ruth 1: 16,17)
I dedicate my whole self to the Lord (Romans 14: 7, 8)
     and I do this deliberately (Joshua 24: 15)
          and sincerely (2 Corinthians 1: 12)
               and freely (Psalm 110: 3)
                    and for ever (Romans 8: 35-39)."

7. The *Hyfforddwr* was translated into English by Thomas Charles' grandson, David Charles, and published in 1867 under the title *The Christian Instructor; or Catechism on the Principles of the Christian Religion*. The fortieth edition of the Welsh work appeared in 1858, and by the end of 1862 five further editions had been called for.

SELECT BIBLIOGRAPHY

(i) *Books in English.*

Davies, Evan. *Revivals in Wales,* London, 1859.

James, John Angell. *Revival of Religion: Its Principles, Necessity, Effects,* London, 1859.

Jones, Owen. *Some of the Great Preachers of Wales,* Second Thousand, London, 1860.

Morgan, J. J. *The '59 Revival in Wales,* Mold, 1909.

Orr, J. Edwin. *The Second Evangelical Awakening in Britain,* London: Edinburgh, 1949.

Phillips, Thomas. *The Welsh Revival,* London, 1860.

Rees, Thomas. *History of Protestant Nonconformity in Wales,* Second Edition, London, 1883.

Miscellaneous Papers on Subjects Relating to Wales, London, 1867.

(ii) *English Periodicals.*

Evangelical Magazine
The Nonconformist
The Revival

(iii) *Welsh Periodicals referred to in the text.*

Yr Annibynwr
Baner Cymru
Y Cyfaill o'r Hen Wlad
Y Diwygiwr
Y Drysorfa
Yr Eurgrawn Wesleyaidd
Y Goleuad
Yr Herald Cymraeg
Seren Gomer
Y Traethodydd

Index

FURTHER TITLES ON REVIVAL FROM THE EVANGELICAL PRESS OF WALES

By Eifion Evans

The Welsh Revival of 1904. A thorough and readable study of the 1904 Revival. Foreword by D. M. Lloyd-Jones.

Fire in the Thatch. A collection of essays and talks on revivals and the people involved.

By Brynmor P. Jones

Voices from the Welsh Revival. Eyewitness testimonies and contemporary accounts of the 1904-05 Revival, woven together into an informative and moving account.

FOR A CURRENT CATALOGUE OF ALL PUBLICATIONS, PLEASE WRITE TO:
THE EVANGELICAL PRESS OF WALES,
BRYNTIRION, BRIDGEND,
MID GLAMORGAN CF31 4DX